Cpa Marketing

How to Get Paid Online for Referring Signups

(How Cpa Marketing is Making Average People Millionaires)

Edith Moody

Published By **Chris David**

Edith Moody

Cpa Marketing: How to Get Paid Online for Referring Signups (How Cpa Marketing is Making Average People Millionaires)

ISBN 978-1-77485-692-5

Legal & Disclaimer

TABLE OF CONTENTS

Introduction

In a world of information overload and misinformation, I am confident that this Book will give you a clear understanding of how CPA marketing and the CPA industry works, regardless of the fact that you are a novice or you've been in the game for years. The biggest challenge that you will encounter in the CPA marketing game is traffic and time. Contrary to what you have heard or read, playing the CPA marketing game is not as easy as it appears. It takes a lot of hard work, dedication and persistence to make a lot of money with CPA offers.

The CPA market is nothing new and has been around since the mid 1990's and brokering traffic from traffic sources like pay per click search engines to CPA offers has been a business for many affiliates for the last ten years

Nowadays, in the field of internet or online marketing, 'affiliate marketing' is a popular term. In affiliate marketing, affiliates can earn money by promoting the products or services of other people or companies in return for a commission on the number of sales made. But have you heard about the new type of affiliate marketing where people get paid even if they don't make a sale?

Yes, it is true. Well, it has been possible by a new wave of affiliate marketing flowing through the web, known as 'CPA Affiliate Marketing' or just "CPA Marketing'. Now, you can earn money online with CPA Marketing.

This Book is a comprehensive guide for anyone looking to learn more about what CPA Marketing and earning from the affiliate program.

Chapter 1: What Is Cpa - A Comprehensive Explanation

CPA, which stands for Cost per Action, is basically a form of affiliate advertisement that is used by almost all companies throughout the world to generate leads for their products. This marketing is done by affiliates who work through their own websites in order to send traffic to the advertiser's website for the product of the company. CPA deals with specific forms of marketing which involve pay per click and pay per lead ads.

Although Google used CPA networking as a major part of their advertising campaign till June 2008, eBay has now taken up this form of marketing and calls it AdContext. CPA is also known as Cost per Acquisition. This makes more sense literally, since affiliate advertisers under CPA networks are paid based on what the advertiser acquires from his or her customers. There is no returning of funds in this sort of advertisement. As long as the entire action is completed by potential customers, affiliates get paid per lead that they provide to the advertiser. This makes it easier and simpler for advertisers to work for their company, as well as for affiliates to work for their advertisers.

Since there are many CPA networks out there and hundreds of affiliates are hired from these networks, advertisers usually have affiliate managers who go through the resume of each of these affiliates and hire only those who have the best lead generation records, or are the most appropriate for a specific line of marketing.

The basic deal with CPA marketing is to generate traffic to the company's website. This job is outsourced by the advertisers of these companies to the affiliates, who in turn get paid in commission depending on the quality of lead generation that they can provide. Affiliates then use various forms of advertising such as banner ads, keywords, article directories, pay per click ads and video ads to attract more traffic for the website.

Companies that sell insurance, credit and/or debit cards, public bonds or even ring tones of cell phones, use CPA networks to build their leads. Affiliates should stay in touch with their managers since the latter are well informed about the latest information regarding the

CPA networks and the newest ideas for this sort of marketing.

Although getting paid $30 for each action that an affiliate is able to generate from potential customers may seem like a cheap bargain for the work that they go through, if they have a handsome customer profile of about 400 to 500, then this amount can multiply into a hefty pay packet per month.

Chapter 2: How To Select The Right Cpa Offer

Once you've been selected by a CPA network, you will need to start to make choices relating to the offers that you are attracted to selling to your online customers. Don't make your choice based just on your likes and dislikes, which means you will need to find the niches that sell more, and that direct high amounts of traffic to enjoy making the huge bucks.

How to Study the Market Competition

The main facet of any business success is the creative intelligence. It really isn't just about who you know, working exhaustively, or luck. No matter what you do, you should always be at your creative best. To be at your best with CPA marketing, you need to do an overload of research to learn what keywords always hit big in the search engines and the ones that are always popular, and you need to watch out for the well-known niches using the many trend sites. Once you know the keywords that are searched extensively. This means that they haven't been used in CPA offers yet, and so you can grab them to use to create your own advertisements for sales.

When you learn that a certain CPA offer is very popular, don't make the mistake of thinking it means that it's a dead end for you. Instead, use the information you've found to get a better understanding of the various products that are tirelessly wanted, and then use them to generate traffic on your website.

The key is to utilize the same methods, the same materials, and the same taglines in making the sales. What matters more than what you sell is how you sell it. There is a huge difference. Your creativity needs to come to forefront and you need to come up with quirky ideas that will appeal to the online shopper.

How do you compare CPA offers?

The main CPA mantra is that your choices should be the ones that are hot, trendy, popular and highest in demand. If you can find that with CPA offers, regardless if they generate a little or a lot of traffic, whether they will fall, or not – you will be making the correct decision with less likelihood of facing defeat.

When you are trying to make the choice regarding which CPA offers you should pick to sell, instead of undertaking individually going through them, which is extremely time consuming, why not take advantage of the many online tools and programs that can quickly help you to located the information you need.

It is a misconception believing that if a CPA offer provides the highest pay then it is the right choice. This way of thinking that can lead to failure. You need to do your research find the niche product that's going to sell over and over again!

Chapter 3: Methods Of Promoting Cpa Offers

There are a number of ways that your CPA promotion can be done. Some of these involve you having your own website while others do not. CPA marketing is very similar to other forms of marketing. At the beginning, you will need to take some time to think about what product you can promote that will fit your niche and where you can market it, where your visitors will either be interested in learning more or in buying a product.

Let's have a look at some of the most commonly used promotional methods for CPA marketing on websites.

1. Sales or Landing Page – This is like a direct sales page and should usually provide additional information on the product. Usually, it's set up to be a hard sale, working hard to get the visitor to click through to the merchant or at least sign up to the site's mailing list. Some sales pages attempt to achieve both of these; however, often it is more beneficial to have one direct path through your landing page. If you have too many options, you could lose more clicks.

2. Review Website – This type of site usually contain three or more products in a specific niche, for instance, weight loss or gardening. There will be a brief introduction to each of the products, followed by a review of the performance of the product, and then often followed with a star rating out of five. Each product is usually ranked in order and contain a link to either a personalized landing page or directly to the merchant's page.

3. Splash Page – Generally, this contains light content with flashy graphics and a punchy headline. The copy encourages the visitors to input their details or to click through to the merchant's site. There is minimal product information provided. These kinds of pages are often used with products that don't need much explanation or that are already known in the marketplace like the iPhone.

4. Fun Landing Page – This is similar to a splash page but simpler. Generally, there is a ⵧuestion with two or more answers, which can be clicked on using the very large dominant buttons. Sometimes a game is used on this kind of page. It isn't the type of page that someone revisits. Its only goal is for your visitors to click-through now.

We've talked about different promotional methods on your website. Of course, there are other methods which will be discussed in the coming chapters but these are one of the most popular.

Chapter 4: How To Select Cpa Offers

Once you decide it's time to start making money with CPA Marketing, you need to browse through the many CPA offers. Start by selecting the best 8-10 CPA networks that you would like to become involved in. Doing this makes it more helpful than just trying to choose one niche and spending all kinds of time doing the research, only to discover that there are all kinds of offers available to you. You can waste a great deal of time and energy, and become more frustrated.

After you choose 8 to 10 best offers, you need to sit down and start to work your way through the markets available online to learn which are the most popular in demand, and to learn which ones are easiest to make the most money. The trick here is to learn what hot topics are being searched for the most in the search engines and news. Google trends are the best place to begin. Go to http://google.com/trends, to find personality news stories. You will need to watch so you don't become sidetracked by these stories. Avoid the personality stories because people aren't interested in personalities when they are reading about the product(s)

After going through these trend sites, you'll have ideas about what is hot and what actually sells the most, along with which niches are closely related to your CPA offers. The best trick to use is to find a sub-niche in a larger niche related to your CPA offers. Don't be scared to make offers available in highly competitive markets. Those where most of the traffic is directed is where you'll do best.

You need to spend a couple of hours researching how you can best create a significant revenue with the CPA network niche you are considering. If you have a number of your own websites, you can continue to keep watching for better offers in the CPA networks. The domain name you use should be related to the niche you are planning to work in.

Now that you have your niche, the work you do will be done upfront. When you are building your site up, you are going to have to change the offers regularly. You may find it tiring to create different websites for different CPA offers, but those e-market affiliates who are experienced can whip up a site in just a few hours using Wordpress. If you want to make it to the top of the earning pool, you'll have to learn how to do this as well.

Chapter 5: The Top 8 Cpa Networks To Join

If you are an affiliate marketer, the first step you need to take to earn good money through online advertising is to join as many CPA networks as possible. Different CPA networks have their own various lead programs that marketers can use. Choose those with high pay per lead and good resell options, as this will lead to higher income generation for you. 8 of the top CPA networks include:

1. MaxBounty

Running a successful CPA Affiliate Network since 2004, MaxBounty has stood the test of time and has become one of the well-known names in the industry. Now, MaxBounty is considered as one of the most popular CPA Affiliate Network. Presently it has thousands of satisfied affiliates that are earning the considerable amount of revenue doing CPA advertising. You can look forward to one of the highest paying affiliate programs from MaxBounty. With MaxBounty, you are bound to get a reliable partner for CPA Affiliate Marketing.

http://promoteam.rurl.me/maxbounty

2. AdCombo

AdCombo is one of the most recognized and fastest growing CPA Affiliate Networks. It is considered as one of the oldest players in the industry and has earned the tag of being one of the most reputed CPA Affiliate Networks. As an Affiliate, you can look forward to a whole range of products and services. They have a wide range of advertisers in different categories. It has been estimated that AdCombo pays almost $ 100M a year to affiliates. Moreover, AdCombo is one of the favorite CPA Affiliate Network for almost every 'Super Affiliate'.

http://promoteam.rurl.me/adcombo

3. PeerFly

With PeerFly, you can look forward to getting excellent affiliate management as far as CPA Affiliate Marketing is concerned. PeerFly has earned the reputation of being one of the fastest growing CPA Affiliate Network in the world. It already has more than 30k publishers spread across 165 countries around the world. As an advertiser, you can look forward to dedicated account managers and lots of other quality services. It runs various CPA offers in different categories from well-known brands. So as a CPA Affiliate you get a wide gamut of choices of affiliate programs from PeerFly.

4. CPALead

CPALead is another leading CPA Affiliate Network that has been running successfully for a considerable length of time. CPALead was previously known as CPAdverts. You can look forward to a whole range of affiliate programs from CPALead. It is a well-known name in the industry and one of the biggest companies running a CPA Affiliate Network. As an affiliate, you can have many quality services from CPALead such as timely payment of bills. Seeing its performance and deliverables in the past recent years, you can expect the CPALead network to continue to grow and flourish in the future, as well.

http://promoteam.rurl.me/cpalead

5. ClickDealer

ClickDealer is one of the greatest CPA affiliate networks, they have a lot of offers with good payout. They have some great affiliate manager who is always ready to help you. For payment, you don't have to worry as ClickDealer offer on-time payment, they also offer direct deposits. If you are looking for a good CPA affiliate network ClickDealer is a great option.

6. CPABuild

CPABuild is another trustworthy and performance driven CPA Affiliate Network coming your way. It figures among the top 10 CPA Affiliate Networks. Moreover, it has been voted as the 5th Best CPA Network so you can very well ascertain its popularity and success in CPA Affiliate Marketing. CPABuild's success springs from the fact that it has based its business on the platform of trust, integrity, respect, and honor. While keeping an eye on the latest technology, CPABuild offers a whole range of quality services to both its advertisers and publishers. You stand to benefit and increase your revenue stream by becoming an advertiser or joining in its various affiliate programs as a publisher.

http://promoteam.rurl.me/cpabuild

7. Wild Affiliates

In its small period of existence, Wild Affiliates has gained the reputation of being one of the fastest growing CPA Affiliate Networks. Moreover, it is now been recognized as one of the largest CPA Affiliate Networks for the casino niche, as well. Wild Affiliates has a whole range of excellent offers and services for its clients with utmost accuracy and dedication. With their 24/7 support team, they guarantee to resolve your queries as soon as possible. So, if you are looking for a reliable, trustworthy, and fast casino-targeted CPA Affiliate Network, then you can surely depend upon the services of Wild Affiliates.

http://promoteam.rurl.me/wildaffiliates

8. Ibex Network

Featuring among the top CPA Affiliate Networks, Ibex Network is another leading CPA Affiliate Network in the world of casino's, gambling in general and games. It has been incorporated with the sole objective of becoming a global performance-based publisher network and is successfully fulfilling its objective. Ibex Network already has thousands of publishers and is able to generate millions of leads/sales per month for its advertising clients. It offers campaigns in almost every segment of categories including top brand casino's that can be promoted through various channels such as email, mobile, social media, web, etc. It has much to offer to both advertisers and publishers. Publishers can look forward to the large gamut of offers, round the clock personalized support, and top payout among others.

http://promoteam.rurl.me/ibex

Chapter 6: Traffic Tactics

There are many forms of traffic that I believe fall into the following four (4) major categories which will all be covered in this section. This section isn't a complete list of all the traffic methods, but rather a quick list of the most common forms of generating traffic to CPA offers.

You can make a ton of money sending traffic to CPA offers from these four traffic models.

The four traffic models are:

• Free Traffic

• Paid Traffic

• Recycled Traffic

• Viral Traffic

Each of these traffic sources could be an entire course on its own. It is not my objective to make this report the encyclopedia of Internet marketing, but rather to point you to resources that I think can help you create traffic.

If you can learn to monetize any of these sources of traffic, you have established the first step towards online success.

FREE TRAFFIC

Natural Search Traffic

Natural search traffic is simply having your web pages indexed by major search engines such as Google, Yahoo or MSN. Back then in the late 1990's, it was very easy to get ranked in the major search engines. Today it is brutally competitive and difficult to get a high ranking for relevant keywords or key phrases.

But it is still possible through some hard work and dedication.

There are two major components to getting your web pages ranked well and they are:

1. On Page Factors

2. Off Page factors

On page, factors include where to place your keywords on your web pages and the keyword density. The obvious methods to improve your on-page factors are:

• include relevant keywords in meta tags

• include relevant keywords in your H1, H2, H3 tags

• include relevant keywords in your image tags (the alt text tag)

• include relevant keywords in your content

Off page factors include other web sites that link back to your web site. There are some things that major search engines look at when analyzing the inbound links to your web site:

• the number of inbound links

• the anchor text used to link to your web site

• the IP address of web site linking to your web site

The off-page factors accounts for 90% of how well ranked your web pages are for relevant keywords in the major search engines.

When you are exchanging links with other web sites, don't simply use your web site name, but rather a keyword that best describes what your web site is all about.

Once you have your website compiled and all the internal links working, you can submit them to the major search engines. With Google, you can use Google Sitemaps, and they will send the Google spider to index your web page right away.

You need to create a sitemap in .xml format for your web site to submit it to Google Sitemaps (http://www.google.com/webmasters/sitemaps).

Social Media Traffic

Social media traffic refers to taking advantage of Web 2.0 sites to generate traffic to the CPA offers that you are promoting. There are essentially two different ways that you can take advantage of Web 2.0 sites.

1. Direct Approach

2. Indirect Approach

Using the direct approach, you can link the CPA offer you are promoting right from the Web 2.0 websites. So, for example, you may create a page on HubPages.com related to home renovations, and then link to home improvement CPA offers from your hub pages.

Using the indirect approach, you use the linking power of web 2.0 websites to build ⍰uality links to your money site (the site that makes you money with CPA offers).

For a thorough guide on Social Media Marketing, check out my ebook "Social Media Marketing: Proven Strategies To Make Big Money Online" at this link: https://www.amazon.com/dp/B074WGKMHR

Forum Traffic

Another method of driving traffic to your CPA offers is to participate in forums that are related to the CPA offer that you would like to promote. Most forums allow you to create a signature file, which means that this signature will be displayed at the end of every forum message that you write.

You can use this area to promote your CPA offer directly or send prospects to your money site and promote your CPA offers from there. For example, if you were promoting a "backyard makeover" CPA offer, you could start participating in forums related to gardening.

The people who are visiting this forum are your ideal prospects who will be interested in the CPA offer and are likely to fill it out.

Article Writing Traffic

Article writing and submission to major article directories is one of the most powerful methods of attracting free traffic to your web sites.

Writing articles or having articles written for your web sites can also help you get better search engine rankings and drive targeted prospects straight to your website.

Some people might start moaning and groaning since they saw "writing articles". No one is really a fan of that though, but the good news is that you can always outsource whatever writeup you want easily. You could also run Google AdSense – a win-win situation.

Now, I am not suggesting that you go "buck wild" and have thousands of articles written. You can start off with outsourcing just a few articles until you find the right article writer.

You will want to test more than one article writer because some just won't give you good quality articles. You need to dig around until you find that right person.

Once you have these articles written by yourself or outsourced, you can easily submit them to free article directories and email announcement lists. This will create some really good targeted traffic to your web site.

Articles are great traffic producers because you get free exposure for your web site. Authors are allowed to include a small biography at the bottom of the article, and this is a great place to put a link back to your web site.

If you are using HTML in your article or signature file at the end of an article, remember to use your most relevant keywords as your anchor text for your link so that you can improve your SEO rankings.

Try Fiverr to find cheap article writers: http://promoteam.rurl.me/fiverr

Domain Name Traffic

This tactic involves registering domain names that are relevant to what you are selling or promoting.

Test and studies have indicated that domain names that include keywords that are searched for have a better ranking than other websites that don't.

Most relevant keywords and keyword phrases have already been registered, but by using a cool software tool called Domain Suggestion Tool, you can still find domain names related to particular keywords that haven't been registered.

Domain   Suggestion   Tool
http://www.domainsuggestiontool.com

You can also pick up expired domain names that still have traffic being sent to them and try to monetize the traffic. A lot of companies concentrate on buying expired domains and simply redirect them to web pages with CPA ads.

These companies are smart in that they know if they can control a vast amount of traffic with expired domains, they can convert this traffic into revenue.

Here are some resources to find expired domains:

ExpiredDomains.com
http://www.expireddomains.com

DeletedDomains.com
http://www.deleteddomains.com

Reciprocal Linking Traffic

Reciprocal linking is simply the link exchange between two websites. Although one-way linking helps you get a better search engine ranking, reciprocal linking still adds some benefit to your ranking.

Most people exchange links now because it helps their web site ranking, but what happened to the good old days when people used to link to each other just to exchange traffic? You will still get traffic from simple link exchanges if the links are shown prominently and not buried deep within the websites.

When trading links between websites, make sure that you are getting a fair deal of traffic for the traffic you will be giving away. It is best to use a tracking script to measure how much traffic you are sending to a link partner versus how much traffic they are sending you.

Here are a few link exchange networks where you can find quality link exchange partners.

Link Partners http://www.linkpartners.com

Value Exchange http://value-exchange.sitesell.com

FollowLike
http://promoteam.rurl.me/followlike

Blogging Traffic

Blogging has become ?uite popular because they seem to rank ?uite well in search engines. Although not as effective as far as 3-5 years ago, blogs still command good rankings because of the fresh content that they bring to search engines. Blogs did well early on because of their optimized site structure. I mean if you look at a blog, it is set up with a clear navigation with every page linked correctly. This is what search engines love.

You can start your blog for free by either using a third-party blogging website or installing free blogging software on your web site.

Blogger (3rd party) http://www.blogger.com

WordPress (standalone software) http://www.wordpress.com

Another new trend in affiliate marketing is the setup of fake blogs to promote CPA offers such as Acai dieting and government grant offers. Some affiliates are creating fake personalities to create social proof for these CPA offers and trying to make it more convincing with fake comments for additional social proof.

Now, this is in no way an endorsement for this type of tactic; this is just to show you a method that is working extremely well for some CPA affiliate marketers.

Joint Venture Traffic

Joint venture traffic is a quick way to leverage the traffic sources (whether it is through email or web traffic) of other webmasters.

The reason why some product launches do well is because they have hundreds of joint venture partners promoting the same program to their email lists. This creates a stampede of traffic to the website of the product launch owner and that equates to mad sales.

If you can find joint venture partners who have highly responsive email lists, they can drive serious traffic to your website.

Most joint ventures involve an affiliate agreement where the joint venture partner takes a percent of the sale price of the product or service being promoted.

So, although joint ventures can create targeted traffic, the cost does come in the form of an affiliate commission.

If you are looking for joint venture partners, the Warrior Internet marketing forum has a section for finding joint venture partners: Warrior   Forum http://www.warriorforum.com/forum/defaul t.asp

Pop Up Traffic

Pop up traffic is a result of someone clicking on a pop-up window that contains an ad for your website or a pop-up window that contains your entire website.

There are hundreds of free pop up/under traffic exchanges on the Internet where you can get free pop under traffic. This traffic does not generally convert very well because these visitors are untargeted.

You will see ads from companies advertising 100,000 visitors to your website for amounts ranging from $10 - $100. This traffic is only good for increasing your web stats or Alexa ranking.

One particularly famous one is Adfly: http://promoteam.rurl.me/adfly

Video Traffic

Video traffic is quickly becoming one of the best methods to drive traffic to websites. Services such as YouTube.com have made it very easy for individuals to upload their videos and share it with their friends and the rest of the YouTube.com community.

A few years ago, many CPA affiliates took advantage of major video sites like YouTube.com by uploading videos from a variety of music artists. They were trying to promote ringtone offers within these videos, and some made a lot of money doing this.

At the end of the video, affiliates would put a message like "Get This Ringtone At" and then link to a CPA ringtone offer. The problem with this method is that they are using copyrighted videos to generate traffic to their ringtone offers and eventually YouTube.com catches on and shuts these accounts down.

This doesn't mean that you still can't use video services to generate traffic to your CPA offers. What you could simply do is first offer quality content in your videos (and this can be something as simple as a PowerPoint presentation) and link back to your money site at the end of the video.

Let me give you an example. You could create a PowerPoint presentation on how to get out of debt. You can find the material for your presentation for free on the Internet by simply googling "how to get out of debt."

Using a tool like Camtasia video, you can record the PowerPoint presentation with your voice as the audio presenting the slides. Simply link back to your money site at the end of a video promoting something related like a "debt" or a "free credit report" CPA offer.

You will generate traffic back to your money site when people go to it after watching the video and if you tag your videos properly with related terms (i.e. debt relief, credit report, debt credit score), you will move up organically on major search engines like Google, Yahoo, and MSN and get additional traffic.

You want to use keyword rich text in the title and description of your video, but yet still have a shocking or eye-catching title. Link to your video from multiple web sites to increase the link value and if you put your video on "auto- start" this will continue to generate views.

In some smaller video communities, if you generate enough views on your video, you can move up on their all-time favorite video rankings.

If you want to create more of personal touch, you can record yourself, or someone talking into the camcorder or web cam on the related topic and then pitch the CPA offer at the end of the video.

Some smart affiliates just create funny or interesting videos that are not directly related to the CPA offer. They are just hoping that their videos will go viral and be seen by a mass audience so that whatever they are pitching at the end of the video is viewed by hundreds of thousands of people.

Here are a few places where you can upload your videos for free for people to watch.

YouTube http://www.youtube.com

Google Videos http://video.google.com

Yahoo Videos http://video.yahoo.com

Viddler http://www.viddler.com

Adhysteria http://www.adhysteria.com

BoFunk http://www.bofunk.com

Esnips http://www.esnips.com

GUBA http://www.guba.com

iviewtube http://www.iviewtube.com

Kewego http://www.kewega.com

LiveVideo http://www.livevideo.com

MegaVideo http://www.megavideo.com

Metacafe http://www.metacafe.com

Motionbox http://www.motionbox.com

Myspace Videos http://vids.myspace.com

Photobucket http://www.photobucket.com

Revver http://www.revver.com

Sharkle http://www.sharkle.com

Spike http://www.spike.com

U2UpFly http://www.u2upfly.com

Vidilife http://www.vidilife.com

ViddYou http://www.viddyou.com

And if you want help making videos: try Fiverr at http://promoteam.rurl.me/fiverr

Podcast Traffic

Podcasts are audio files that are automatically delivered directly to your desktop computer, and can be transferred to a podcast. The difference is its ability to be syndicated, subscribed to, and downloaded automatically when new content is added. You can create audio files related to CPA offers and distribute them as podcasts so that they are passed onto users who are interested in the content.

For example, you could create podcasts related to celebrity gossip and promote ringtones at the end of each audio podcast.

Software Traffic

If you have any programming skills or know where to outsource cheap programmers, you could easily create a software program and spread it virally. An example would be Fiverr: http://promoteam.rurl.me/fiverr

Within the software, itself, you could promote CPA offers using banners or text links. For example, if you created a software program such as a dieting diary, you could promote dieting CPA offers with the software.

You can then upload your new software program to the many software sharing web services.

Here are just a few:

Upload.com http://upload.cnet.com

Easy-Share.com http://www.easy-share.com

Facebook Applications Traffic

Facebook allows developers to create applications to be used by the Facebook community. The potential is incredible because it offers developers the opportunity to access to the over 100 million Facebook users and make money.

A lot of developers have incorporated CPA offers into their Facebook applications and made obscene amounts of money. Some claim to have made as much as $1 million per week monetizing Facebook applications and CPA offers.

Okay, let's move on to the paid traffic sources.

PAID TRAFFIC

Pay Per Click Search Engine Traffic

Yahoo Search Marketing (formerly known as Overture and Goto) was the first successful pay per click search engine to come on to the scene in 1999.

Before 1999, many companies and individuals resisted the bid per placement idea, and that is why Open Text and AltaVista both failed in their attempts to charge advertisers for rankings a few years before Goto.com (now Yahoo Search Marketing) came onto the scene.

The reason why the market initially had resisted the idea of using a search engine that charged for placement was because they felt the results would be tainted and irrelevant.

Today, however, many pay per click search engines only allow advertisers to bid on relevant keywords to keep the quality of their search results high. For example, Google AdWords lets their users decide what ads are relevant by assigning a click-thru rate on paid advertisements.

On pay per click search engines, advertisers simply bid on keywords that are related to their product or service. Their ad listings will be displayed when a prospective customer types any of those keywords into a search form. Rankings on the major pay per click search engines are based primarily on the bid price and the click-through rate on the advertiser's ads. The nice thing about pay per click search engines is that you are in control, and you decide the maximum price you want to pay for a visitor to be directed to your web site.

Here are some of the big ad companies that will give you PPC traffic.

Google AdWords http://adwords.google.com

Yahoo Search Marketing http://searchmarketing.yahoo.com

MSN Adcenter http://adcenter.microsoft.com

Facebook http://www.facebook.com/advertising

MySpace http://advertise.myspace.com

Publisher Network Traffic

Contextual networks allow advertisers to place their text ads on thousands of websites that participate in the contextual ad network's publisher program. Most times, people refer contextual networks as mini Google AdSense services because they are the same thing.

Anytime someone clicks on an advertiser's ad on a publisher's website; the publisher is paid a percentage of the click cost. The contextual network keeps the remaining percent, and the advertiser is charged per click.

The key to driving targeted traffic from contextual networks is based on how well they can place targeted ads on the web sites in their publisher program. The better their ability to match the ads with the content on the web site, the better-quality traffic you will get.

Here are a few major contextual networks where you can buy traffic from:

Clicksor http://www.Clicksor.com

AdBrite http://www.AdBrite.com

ValidClick http://www.ValidClick.com

Pulse360 http://www.pulse360.com

Text Link Traffic

Another source of paid traffic is buying static text links on various websites. Buying static text links on websites can help you increase the number of one-way links that are pointing towards your website.

The key is to finding targeted websites that are interested in selling static links on their web site. There are web services that work as middlemen for buyers and sellers of text links.

Buying text links can help with search engine optimization by increasing your web sites rank and creating direct links for traffic back to your web site. Remember that 90% of the success of your web pages on organic search engines is related to off page factors such as the number of one-way links coming in.

Here are two major web services where you can buy static text links:

Text Link Ads http://www.Text-Link-Ads.com

Text Link Brokers http://www.TextLinkBrokers.com

Co-Registration Traffic

Co-registration is simply buying leads from companies that collect them from co-registration forms. A lot of companies can provide you with a large number of single opt-in leads on a daily basis.

Sometimes as high as 100,000 leads per day!

The price for co-registration leads varies and can start as low as $0.10 an email address. You need to take these leads and convert them into traffic. It is smart to go with a co-registration service that automatically puts these leads into an autoresponder in real-time so you can get the prospect while they are hot.

You can either direct them to your web site in an autoresponder email or try to sell directly to them in the email.

Banner Traffic

Are banners dead? Heck, no!

If you can create eye-catching banners, you can still drive a good amount of traffic to your websites. Creating text banners can out-pull image banners by up to three times.

You simply create a killer headline on your banner and try to entice the reader to click on the banner. Adding the keywords "Click Here" somewhere on your banner will almost always increase the click-thru rate.

You can literally start getting millions of banner impressions by using the site-targeting feature in Google Adwords. If you have a Google AdWords account, instead of setting up a keyword-targeting campaign, you can set up a site- targeting campaign.

You select the web sites that you want your banner to appear on, and you can test and track to see what web sites pull the best conversions for what you are promoting.

Google charges as low as $0.25 for every 1,000 banner impressions so you can test and track without losing your shirt.

Google Adwords

https://adwords.google.com

Other places where you can buy banner traffic are:

Casale Media http://www.casalemedia.com

ValueClick http://www.valueclick.com

And if you need help creating an awesome banner, try Fiverr: http://promoteam.rurl.me/fiverr

Media Buys Traffic

Media buying simply refers to buying bulk advertising space for mass advertising campaigns. You can generate a ton of traffic from doing media buys, but it can get very expensive.

The key to making media buys work well is to make sure that you have thoroughly tested the response rate of the landing page so that you have a general idea of what the conversion rate will be.

Okay, let's move on to recycled traffic...

RECYCLED TRAFFIC

Email Traffic

One of the first things that you should be concentrating on when building traffic is to have a system set up to capture email addresses of the visitors that come to your web site.

This way you can recycle this traffic by directing them back to your website through email messages. Recycled traffic is virtually free and can help brand your web site with prospects.

The first thing that you want to do is create a pop-up window on your website that grabs the attention of your visitors as soon as they arrive at your website.

Popup windows can increase your opt-in rate dramatically compared to a simple opt-in form on your web site.

As much as you may hate pop-up windows, the fact is that they work.

Internal Banner Traffic

This strategy is one of the biggest sources of recycled traffic and continues to move hundreds of visitors between network of websites every day.

This works by creating banners that only link back to websites that you own or control. This means that you are keeping your visitors on your network of websites. What this does is increase the likelihood of someone completing a CPA offer that you will be promoting on your website.

The longer you can keep traffic moving within your websites, you will see a direct relation to how much money you will make.

You can download a free script called OpenX that will completely run your internal banner network and provide you with powerful statistics on what is working and what is not.

OpenX http://www.openx.com

Forum Recycled Traffic

Forums are a great way to attract visitors back to your websites. People like to converse with each other about niche topics and will be willing to come back to your web site if you give them the ability to do so.

There are many free forum scripts on the Internet, and a perfect free one is PHP Forums, which is available at:

PHP Forum http://www.phpforum.com

You can even place banners in your forum pulled directly from the CPA networks. For example, if you are running a dieting related forum, you can run various CPA dieting offers.

Surveys and Poll Traffic

People love to express their opinion or take surveys. That is why programs that offer to pay people to take surveys do so well. By creating a poll on your website, you can encourage visitors to come back to your website to view the results. On these polls, you can run banners or text links for CPA offers.

You can create polls that are targeted towards certain CPA offers so that you are targeting the right prospects. You can go to any website that offers free CGI scripts and find a polling script fairly quickly to add to your web site. Here are some survey and poll services:

PollDaddy.com http://www.polldaddy.com

SurveyMonkey.com
http://www.surveymonkey.com

Now, let's move on to one of the best and most efficient form of traffic.

VIRAL TRAFFIC

This is the most powerful form of traffic that you could generate because it is free most of the time and grows virally.

Five main pillars are the foundation for a successful viral marketing campaign:

Pillar #1: Innovative Product or Service

Viral marketing works best when you give or sell an innovative product or service that people want. Hotmail was the first web service to give away free web-based email accounts.

You don't necessarily have to reinvent the wheel; you can still give or sell a product or service that is not new and still be successful. You just will not be as successful as if you had been the first person to promote the product or service in the market.

Viral marketing programs that give away things for free usually reach the most number of people, especially if the product or service is of high-perceived value. Other common examples of valuable products and services on the Internet are free email, free eBooks, free reports, and free postcards.

Pillar #2: Ease of Transfer

A virus can only survive when it can transfer easily from one host to another. Whatever product or service you decide to promote using a viral marketing campaign, it must be easily transferable.

For example, chain letters thrive on the Internet because they can easily be transmitted via email. Digital products such as e-books, reports, and software programs spread like wildfire because they are easy to copy and transfer.

Pillar #3: Motivational Factor

The product or service must motivate the user to pass it on to others. For example, electronic greeting cards thrive on viral marketing because people are motivated to send greeting cards to each other.

Numerous motivational behaviors can be exploited with viral marketing strategies to ensure the transmission of a marketing message. One of the most common motivational factors is the opportunity to make money. This is why many network marketing companies have become successful.

Pillar #4: Third-Party Resources

Viral marketing campaigns take advantage of other people's resources. For example, authors who give away free e-books or software and allow users to spread them around are taking advantage of other people's resources.

It is the user who is paying for the list server and bandwidth costs when he or she sends out these free e-book or software to their ezine.

Pillar #5: Scalability

The failure of many companies that run a viral marketing campaign is the fact that they could not scale from small to large quickly enough, killing the host in the end.

For example, at one point, Hotmail could not handle all the email accounts that were being registered and used. They simply did not have the resources to manage the explosion in new accounts.

There is a good chance that they could have ended up going out of business if Microsoft had not bought them out and infused their resources into the Hotmail service.

This is also the primary reason why a lot of hit exchanges and banner exchanges crashed in the past. They could not handle the bandwidth on their servers, and their services ultimately came to a screeching halt - causing many of their users to abandon them.

If you create a viral marketing campaign that is dependent on your resources, you must plan ahead to handle additional growth.

Developing a viral marketing campaign will be pointless if it ends up killing the host while it expands exponentially.

Social Networking Traffic

Websites like MySpace.com and YouTube.com command enormous amounts of traffic because of their users. They have created social networks that allow people to get in touch with each other more easily and share items such as videos.

The thing that makes these websites so powerful is that they are completely user driven. It is the community that builds that website and content. It is the users that are spreading the message and telling their friends to join the community. This is the viral aspect of social networking websites.

If you are serious about starting your social networking site that grows virally, you can get free scripts on the Internet that will allow you to build your own mini Myspace. Once you build your community, you can place targeted CPA offers and generate CPA commissions from all the free traffic.

Ning http://www.ning.com

Dolphin Smart Community Builder http://ww.boonex.com/products/dolphin

For a thorough guide on Social Media Marketing, check out my ebook "Social Media Marketing: Proven Strategies To Make Big Money Online" at this link: https://www.amazon.com/dp/B074WGKMHR

Tell A Friend Script Traffic

"Tell a friend" scripts are a powerful viral marketing tool because it encourages people to let their friends know about your website. People are more inclined to visit your web site when a trusted friend recommends it to them.

If you have your website, you should take advantage of a script like this because you can promote your CPA offers within emails that are sent out from the script and capture more leads.

FreeTellAFriend.com
http://www.freetellafriend.com

Viral Report Traffic

Many people create reports and give them away hoping that people will pass them around. Some offer resells rights, and others grant users permission to give them away for free or use them as bonuses for their products. This report that you are reading is a prime example of a viral report.

Chapter 7: Why Do So Many Cpa Affiliate Marketers Fail?

You're ready to quit your day job – tell your boss to take a hike and head on over to the online world to take advantage of internet marketing. You sit into the wee hours of the morning obsessed. Everything sounds amazing from Facebook money making to email marketing to making money on YouTube. It makes sense to you, so you buy a course. This is like the gold rush of the 1800s and you are about to strike it rich - The next thing you know, your brain runs out of room for the clutter, your wallet is empty and your dream dies before it ever gets off the ground. Yet you could have avoided all of this. You really could have struck gold – so what did you do wrong?

You Quit Too Soon – It's Also What CPA Marketers Do Far Too Often

If you don't buy a ticket to the lottery, you can't win. Never have truer words been said. The prize for internet marketing isn't just big – it's huge – its life changing. If you want to succeed, you need to 'never say die.' That attitude will guarantee that you will eventually enjoy success. Hang on to your day job for a little longer, put your energy into getting your CPA marketing off the ground, and then you will be ready to quit with success already in your pocket.

Running before You Walk

In other words, excess rush, which will reduce your chances of making decent money online. It's much better to work towards making and extra $20 a day than to go too BIG right from the beginning, spreading yourself too thin because you believe that you need to be making $100 a day right now! Slow and steady really does win the online race. That's how you will enjoy successful CPA marketing.

Is Your CPA Marketing Actually Working?

If you want to be successful working online, you need to be ready to test and tweak everything you do in an ongoing fashion. It's common for newbies in the CPA marketing world to be reckless and this often results in some profit, but the problem is that you aren't able to pinpoint just how or why you made the money so it's impossible to duplicate your results. You need to be smarter than that – you need to keep good notes. Try something – wait – evaluate.

CPA Marketing Done Right Means Success

Do it right, take your time, be patient, be flexible and you can enjoy CPA Marketing success.

Chapter 8: 6 Steps To Choose The Best Cpa Offer To Promote

If you want to create the best CPA offer to promote, follow these six steps.

Step #1

Picking a niche that you think you can promote takes a little strategy. It's good to choose a niche that you have some knowledge in, because this can help to reduce the time it takes to get going. If you aren't sure at the beginning, don't worry, you will develop this skill you need over time. If you are new to this, I would recommend that you look for something in the payout range of $2 to $10. This will help keep your testing cheap. The last thing you need to consider is the source of your traffic. Some traffic sources will not allow some types of offers or they might not do well with a certain offer.

Step #2

Find your niche and then seek out the top offers that have on average the highest network EPCs. List the top few offers on the CPA networks you have joined. You shouldn't compare network average EPCs between the various CPA networks. There are far too many variables and so your comparisons will not be valid or provide you with good insight.

Step #3

Your affiliate managers are there to help you and to answer your questions. One of the thing you need to ask is what offers your affiliate manager feels is doing the best in your particular niche.

Step #4

Take the time to have a look at each offer in-depth. Look at things like the design, the landing page copy, the consumer price; if it is a direct sale offer and just how you feel overall about the design. What is your gut feeling? Take advantage of Alexa.com, where you can check out how much traffic the offer URL gets. This information can help you tell if the offer is new or if it's been around for some time. Being new should not be a deal breaker but it is something to be aware of and to pay attention to. Think about how easily or quickly you can make a good landing page.

Step #5

Pick two or three top offers that you are going to split test. It is important that you test each offer for a minimum of 100 clicks before you make any decisions.

Step #6

This step is only necessary if your offer requires you to have approval. You will then need to reach out to the affiliate manager or the person that approves the applications. Don't be afraid to pick up the phone and call them as a follow up to your approval request. Almost all are going to call you to ensure you are a legitimate business, so beat them to it.

Answer all questions you are asked, or perhaps, if you have any questions too, they would be willing to help.

Chapter 9: How To Join A Cpa Network

Joining a CPA Network is more difficult than joining a basic market affiliating program. But if you know how this system works, you can certainly create your own opportunity especially using these steps:

#1 Choose one or more networks that you would like to join. You definitely want to choose more than one CPA Network. There is a wide collection of networks to choose and apply (You can even refer to the Chapter 5 section of this book) in order to land up with the best offers, since more applications means an increase in your options. Make sure that you take the time to compare the options and features of each of the networks since different networks will have different pay for the same offers. Choose the network that best seems to suits your needs.

#2 Fill out the submission form and try your best to answer all the questions as best that you can. The network managers are interested in knowing about your website, how much traffic you generate, the methods you wish to use to make online sales, etc. Don't be scared by these questions. Just be honest. If you have extremely limited knowledge in this business scope, it will not be the end of the world. They realize that you have to start somewhere, so just be honest in answering the questions.

#3 After you submit the forms, expect to wait for a week or sometimes even longer before you hear from anyone. If you want to speed things up, all you need to do is give the CPA network a call and you watch how quickly you get approved to their CPA network! When the managers see how enthusiastic you are to get the job, they will be impressed enough to have you working for them immediately!

#4 You might discover that some CPA networks are difficult to join. In these situations, it is better that you tell them what your business plan looks like to promote their offers. This will allow them to see that you have the initiative to make sure everything is in order. This will make them far more likely that they accept you right away!

In rare occasion where these tricks fail to work, you can have a successful CPA marketer put a good word in for you. Begin to work in those networks that you have been accepted, and then you can begin to build more experience. It doesn't hurt to build on your contacts. Before you know it, you will start to work as a CPA marketer!

Business is all about making money. So as long as you can keep the green flowing to a business, they'll be interested in having you on board.

Chapter 10: The #1 Fear In Cpa Marketing

You are reading this because you want to know what the main fear is when it comes to CPA marketing. If you are new to CPA marketing, it can be kind of scary. Don't let the fear of you losing your money be the reason for stopping yourself from making money. Success is really based on making sure you test – test – test – stay on top of what you are doing, know what's working and what's not working.

The fear of failure is the number one fear in CPA marketing. It's also what will stop most people dead in their tracks before they even get started. After all, if you haven't started, you can't fail, of course, you also can't succeed. Having this mentality is not the mentality for success.

Perhaps it's due to lack of self confidence, or maybe you have low self esteem. Whatever the reason, you need to address it if you want to enjoy success in CPA marketing. You need to be patient and you need to be willing to step out of your comfort zone. Chances are for most of you considering CPA marketing as beginners, it's something you've not done before. So it's going to take some time for you to be comfortable. The reality is that you are likely to fail your first go round at CPA marketing. After all, you really do need to be bad before you can be good and then when you really understand the 'game' you'll be great. Keep this in mind. It's part of your journey to success.

The message here is if at first you don't succeed and you fail, don't walk away. Get back up, dust yourself off, and try again! Can you imagine what the world would be like if we were all successful the first time we tried something? The thing is that many will fail and then never try again. Instead, they'll head back to the life they know. What you need to remember is that you are working towards a goal, towards successful CPA marketing that can create a steady income flow for you and change your life. The best way for you to deal with your strong fear of failure is to have a very strong focus. When you have something that you are working towards with purpose, it will help to keep you motivated and you will be much less likely to quit.

CPA marketing has great potential; don't let fear stop you from experiencing the revenue it can generate.

Chapter 11: The Benefits Of Cpa Marketing

CPA marketing – if you aren't familiar with it now is a good time to learn more about it. You may have used Google AdSense or perhaps you have used sites like Clickbank. If you are unhappy with the results, you aren't alone. CPA marketing is different, and it is one of the best as an affiliate that you can monetize your site(s).

CPA or Cost Per Action Marketing is a simple system. When someone clicks on your affiliate link and he/she completes the necessary action, you get paid. The necessary action, can be many different things, but usually involves:

* Getting a quote or estimate

* Filling out a form

* Buying something

* Signing up for a free trial

These are the main actions required for you to get paid with CPA Marketing. But why should you choose CPA marketing over some of the other options? Glad you asked!

Why Use CPA Marketing

There are two key reasons to consider using CPA Marketing rather than AdSense, banner advertising or other affiliate marketing strategies. The most important is simply that you are higher on the value chain and the higher the value the more money you are likely to make from your site. That means you'll see higher ROI on CPA Marketing than you will on other forms of marketing. Physical products have up to ten different companies involved in that product, such as warehouses, distributors, and suppliers. It's why if you are an Amazon Associate selling a $3000 computer, you only make about $100.

The second reason to consider CPA Marketing is that it is an integrated form of advertising. That means there is no need for you to make your site look ugly with banner ads and AdSense blocks. CPA Marketing will seamlessly integrate with your site. The offers fit in with your content and blends in with your site. This means that you can easily run a branded website that looks clean and professional, while you can still benefit from CPCs, RPMs, and CTR.

CPR Marketing provides you with a seamless way to integrate advertising. You start by finding an offer that you are interested in and that you feel will work well with your website. There are all kinds of CPA networks out there; each has hundreds of different offers, so you should not have a problem finding an offer that works well with your site.

Chapter 12: What Are Cpa Offers?

CPA simply stands for "Cost Per Action" or "Cash

Per Action." Advertisers might use these

programs to increase their sales, attract sales

leads, get more visitors to their own websites,

or even increase their brand exposure.

To accomplish this, the advertisers establish an affiliate program, and they recruit affiliates who they will pay a specified amount each time one of these actions gets performed.

Typically, there are 4 kinds of CPA programs:

• CPS: Cost Per Sale programs pay affiliates per sale. The pay might be a fixed amount or a percentage of the sale.

• CPL: Advertisers pay a fixed amount for attracting people who fill out a lead form. These might be sales leads or simply subscribers to an email list.

• CPC: These programs pay affiliates for each click to a website.

• CPM: Some advertisers even pay affiliates for the number of advertising impressions that they can generate.

How Do Affiliates Post Advertisements?

Affiliate programs usually provide their affiliates with a variety of linking codes. These can be cut and pasted onto various websites. The code may be for a text or banner advertisements, and most programs have a variety of different advertisement to choose from.

Which Type of CPA Offers Generate The Most Money For Affiliates?

This is a tough question to answer, but the real answer is it depends. The best-performing answers really depend upon the affiliate program, your visitors, and your niche.

Lead Programs

In my own experience, for example, lead programs performed very well in financial niches where the products where very expensive, complex, and probably required more than just a website to sell. Financial advisers, insurance agents, and other financial professionals could make use of these leads as a way to contact consumers to explain their programs, but it was hard to just "sell" the products from a website.

You can find several lead programs on the Internet, and the right one really depends upon the type of online traffic that you hope to attract or already have.

Cost Per Sale Programs

For physical goods, CPS programs might be a better choice. I found that when people searched online for a book or a book case, they did not really need to ask any questions, but they simply wanted to find the right product and buy it.

Amazon is one of the most popular examples of a CPS affiliate program, and the site sells just about anything that you can imagine, so you might want to take a look. You can also find some good networks that contain a lot of different CPS programs, and one example is a company called Share-A-Sale.

Can You Make Money With Cost Per Click Programs?

Don't discount the money you can make from good CPC programs either. Typically, the revenue that you can generate from a click depends upon the niche. Niches like insurance, medical, and law tend to pay very well. Niches for cheaper products and services will not pay as well, but you might be able to generate a lot more clicks in a less-competitive field. Adsense is probably the most well-known

example of a CPC program. Some people

say they can't make any money with this

program because the clicks only pay

pennies. However, if you stick to higher

paying niches, you are likely to get a dollar

or a few dollars per click, and this money

can add up fast.

Cost Per Impression Programs

Some companies will pay just for displaying their advertisements. They usually pay per thousand impressions, and they do not usually pay a lot. These programs are probably best when you have access to a lot of traffic, but you do not really think your traffic is of the type of actually buy anything or fill out a lead form.

For example, if you have a site that appeals to young people without credit cards, but you have quite a bit of that traffic, you might see how a cost per impression program does for you.

There Is Not A Best CPA Offer, But There Are Good Ones!

You will always need to test a variety of different programs. For example, you might try to capture leads on a page, but you might also have another program displayed further down the page to capture a buck or two from people who aren't filling out lead forms that day.

Which CPA Offers Should You

 Choose?

One of the most difficult tasks you will have is selecting the right CPA offers to promote. Trust me, you won't have any trouble finding CPA offers. There are thousands of them out there. But you need to find offers that your traffic will be interested in, pay well, and are offered by well-run affiliate programs.

What Ads Are Your Competitor's Running?

Can you find websites and blogs in similar niches to your own? You might look at some established sites to see what companies they promote. See, what they are actually doing, and don't go by what some blog posts says that they do.

Be Wary Of The CPA-Offer-Of-The-Day

A lot of times, you will find people posting about affiliate programs in order to generate signups, so they can get second-tier commissions. It would be sensible if bloggers would only promote offers that they knew were good, and some bloggers do this. But you will find that some bloggers simply want to post a lot of offers because they hope something will stick. Again, you might see what offers popular blogs run, but don't pick the offer-of-the-day that they happen to be announcing in a post.

Choose Affiliate Programs From Credible CPA Networks

Your own website or blog might be in a unique niche like Texas gardening or alternative energy. This is fine, but you will probably find that the big offers are for things like dating sites or fat burning. However, there are some large networks that have programs for almost anything under the sun --

and that includes solar power or garden seeds -- thing you do find under the sun!

ShareaSale: This is a well known affiliate program that has just about any sort of program that you can imagine. Their programs do run the gamut from plumbing supplies to solar energy system suppliers to natural remedies.

Once you sign up for this network, you can also find out a lot about different advertisers. For example, you can find out how much people are making who run the ads. Other promoter's results might not reflect yours. You could do better than average or worse than average. It all depends upon the quality of your traffic and how closely the advertiser matches your niche.

ShareASale is not the only network. Commission Junction is another popular one, and there are others. Both of these networks have a lot of choices, and they also have some well-known companies that use them to run their affiliate programs. Promoting companies that your visitor has already heard of is a lot easier than introducing consumers to an unknown company.

Everybody Ends Up At Amazon Sooner Or Later

Of course, Amazon.com runs the granddaddy affiliate program. The only problem with Amazon is that commissions start at only around 4 percent. You can surely find much higher payouts elsewhere. But a lot of online publishers like to promote

Amazon because the site contains just about anything that anybody could ever thing of buying. Also, almost everybody has already heard of Amazon and trusts them to deliver their products.

Plus, you get paid on anything your visitor buys. You might be promoting the new release of a book, but if your customer clicks through and buys a big TV set, you have just had a nice payday! In fact, a lot of the online publishers who do favor Amazon only concentrate on selling big-ticket items.

• Getting paid four percent of a $12.00 book is not exciting.

• But getting paid four percent of a $1,500 fishing boat or a $16,000 3D Smart TV is better.

Yeah, I'm still waiting to sell a $16,000 TV. But I can tell you that I've run sites for readers with reviews of Amazon books, and I've been credited for plenty of sales of more expensive items. It would be worth it get paid .50 for a book sale unless I can do a lot of volume, but mix that in with a couple of bigger purchases a day, and I can have a nice payday.

Is Adsense Sense Or Cents?

Again, it all depends upon your website. If you promote higher paying niches, you may find that your clicks add up to hundreds of dollars a day. Unless you have a massive amount of high quality traffic, it can be tough to make a living in a lower-paying niche with Adsense.

Where To Advertise CPA Offers

CPA offers are an excellent means of entering into the lucrative world of online marketing. When starting out, many people base the majority of their business around their own personal website.

A personal website is appealing as it allows you to control all aspects of the experience. Once the viewer comes to your site, you are in control of what they see and how they interact with the site.

Because of this, it can be comforting to know that customers are viewing your offers in the manner you deem best suited. However, finding ways to get people onto your website can be difficult, as well as limiting.

There are many different places where you can promote your CPA offers, allowing you to step outside of your comfort zone and find new, exciting and financially rewarding ways to interact with your viewers. When you no longer limit yourself to any one website, you open up you potential customer base. Choosing to interact with people in a variety of settings can make a real difference when it comes to the amount of money you are able to make, and how scalable your business becomes.

Social Media Sites

Perhaps the most obvious avenue for potential revenue is social media. Following a boom in internet activity in the last decade, more and more social media networks have sprung up.

Taking advantage of everything on offer ensures that a large number of people will be able to see your CPA offers, and better yet, share them among their friends. Each network is built slightly differently, so it may be important to tailor your offer to suit the site on which you wish to promote.

The key is to create an appeal, something which will make viewers want to action your offers.

The beauty of social networking is that the web of interest is already created; once you have a access to one view, they may choose to pass that on to their friends, creating interest beyond the initial viewing which is not nearly as likely on your own personal site.

Another advantage of social networks over personal websites is that much of the operating costs are borne by the social network itself.

Rather than having to pay for hosting or design, you can simply enter your information into prebuilt designs and allow the site itself to handle any technical qualms. This allows you to take advantage of a reliable, scalable platform without having to maintain your own site.

Forums

In a similar vein, dedicated forums can provide an excellent opportunity for viewers to see and action your CPA offers. Forums are typically smaller, more dedicated communities than the wider appeal of social networks.

As such, it can be important to target your offers accordingly. If, when you log onto a forum, you can see that much of the conversation happens to be dedicated to an offer which you have an affiliation with, then it becomes the perfect place to advertise.

The benefit of a forum is that it offers a pool of dedicated potential, allowing you to pick and choose where to share your offers based on the relevance and potential interest.

Like social networks, there is little need for running costs to be accounted for, with the majority being handled by the site itself.

The difference between forums and social networks, however, might be that forums require a greater level of interaction with the existing members.

However, if you are willing to put the time into fostering relationships within the right communities, you can find a wealth of potential revenue with the right forum.

Apps

A relatively new opportunity to promote your CPA offers is to be found in apps. Thanks to the continuing success of the smartphone, many people now have access to apps on the go.

By building your CPA offers into apps, or promoting them via apps, you can reach a large number of people.

The chief benefit here is the mobile nature of the delivery system: a mobile app does not necessarily dictate that a person needs to be sat at their desk to become involved with your CPA. Thanks to apps, you can now find new ways to promote your CPA anywhere in the world!

Make Sure That Your CPA Offers

Perform

You are going to invest some work in your CPA campaigns, so make certain that those CPA offers pay you back. Even very similar looking offers can perform very differently, so it is critical to take the time to test them. Additionally, some offers might do find when you include them on your website, but they might not work as well with social media sites or email campaigns.

I doubt that anybody has a perfect track record of guessing which offers will do the best, and that is why professional marketers are always testing different offers. However, one very common newbie mistake is a lack of tracking or testing.

I have heard so many new marketers complain that they never make any money. I ask them how much traffic they have, and these new marketers have no idea. These newbies might want to blame the affiliate program, but the problem might be that they have almost no traffic to send to the program. You really need to base your judgements upon a large enough sample of data too.

Don't be afraid of the word "test." You are not the one being tested, but the affiliate programs that you chose to use are. There are actually plenty of simple tools that you can use to figure out how well different offers perform when you include them on your website, social networking pages, or email marketing campaigns.

What Should You Track?

When it comes down to it, you really just want to know which campaigns are more profitable. For example, I have tested PPC vs. PPL programs on financial sites. The lead programs might offer $5 or more a lead, so they seem like they pay much better than a click program that pays out $1 per visitor that I can send.

Example Results:

• Conversion rate of 20% on leads • 100 visitors a day

• Average of $50 per 100 visitors with PPC Which is better. Well, I got 20 leads out of 100 visitors, and those are very good results. Those twenty visitors earned me $100. I only earned $50 when I used a PPC strategy. But that was just the results from one page.

In other cases, I might find niches that pay out much better than $1 a click. Indeed, my highest paying Adsense click ever was $17, but those don't happen every day. Still, there are niches where clicks can payout $3 or more. If you changed the math to include a higher paying PPC program, you can see that it would be a clear winner.

That's Why You Have To Test

The thing is that you will never know how much you can earn per click, what you conversion rate will be, or which program you should use unless you run them for awhile with live traffic.

Testing Tools

A lot of times, you can gather enough information by simply using a traffic counter and your affiliate program's statistics page. This might be enough when you are getting started. You would be surprised how many affiliate marketers never even take the time to do this. But how can they ever figure out why they aren't making sales if they don't even know if they have any traffic?

Google Analytics can provide most of the statistics you need about your traffic. You simply incorporate a small piece of code on each page of your site, and you will see who visits, how they found your site, and a lot more.

Some affiliate programs even have conversion scripts that you can also include on your website. These work with Google Analytics to show you exactly which page, and even which visitor, produced a sale. This is a good way to get really accurate information about your traffic statistics, sales, and conversion rates.

You may never need more than this, but if you really want to fine-tune your statistics, you can purchase professional tracking tools too. These might be particularly important if you are paying a lot of money for your traffic, or if you have some reason to doubt your affiliate program's statistics.

A product called Prosper202 can be used to track both traffic to your website, clicks through to an advertiser, and conversions.

You actually host this software on your servers. This is important to many marketers who have concerns about letting anybody else have access to their data.

Can You Make Money By Getting

Other People To Promote CPA Offers?

After you have a little experience with different CPA offers, you might explore another way to make money. A lot of affiliate programs have second or even third tier payout schemes. This means that you can recruit other people to promote the CPA offer, and you can make a little money whenever they make money.

Sometimes that money can add up. In fact, some marketers spend almost 100 percent of their time recruiting. Sure, you make more money if you get the sale. But getting a smaller percentage of many people's sales might work out for you.

Keys To Making Money By Recruiting

1. Only promote offers that you have actually tested or have some reason to believe are good.

2. Offer to help people you recruit get started with some good tips about how to promote the offer.

3. Spend time with other affiliates who are actually putting in some effort.

Of course, you only get paid when other people also make money, so it only makes sense to promote offers that you have tested yourself.

I don't really understand why some marketers will promote a new offer every day when it is obvious that they cannot have test them all. I guess they figure that they can throw enough things against the wall, and something will stick.

If you have developed a good strategy for promoting an offer, you might not be that eager to give it away. You will still make more money when you push the offer yourself than you will if one of your recruits does. You have to use your common sense, but it might be helpful if you let a few tips drop, so they could get started on the right foot. After all, you only make money from your recruits when you make money.

Be careful of spending to much time coaching others. In my experience, about 20 percent of affiliates that I recruit ever actually push any business. The rest won't be worth your time.

It's great to help people out, but you need to manage your time wisely. You might offer to help your recruits after they have demonstrated that they can make a sale or two.

How To Find Other Affiliates To Recruit

There are a lot of good ways to find people to push products.

• Start your own marketing blog.

• Hang out on webmaster forums.

• Find social media groups with Internet marketers. You might eventually want to start your own marketing blog. You can always monetize it by advertising products and services that affiliate marketers might use. Of course, you can also promote affiliate programs that pay you to recruit people.

Some marketers make more money off of their second and third tier commissions than they make off of their own sales. It's great work if you can do it.

You should also consider networking on webmaster forums. However, you have to be careful because those forums can be a tremendous waste of time if you don't stick to business.

You might not be able to directly promote your offer, but you might be able to put a link in your forum signature. Make a few helpful posts and present yourself as a credible resource. You are bound to find other marketers who are interested in finding good affiliate programs to promote.

You can also find affiliate marketing groups on social network. Consider checking Facebook or LinkedIn. Both of these large social networking sites have a lot of groups where marketers hang out, and they can also be great ways to make connections.

Just like you need to be careful to manage your time well on forums, be careful you don't waste too much time on social sites. You can network and do business, but you can also find yourself wasting a lot of time.

Should You Spend Time Recruiting Affiliates?

Actually, it is probably a good idea trying to recruit affiliates for good programs.

Who wouldn't want to sit back and earn

money from the work that other people do?

In any case, you might even want to develop

your own product some day, and you can use

your list of contacts to help you.

CPA Offers To Avoid

Cost Per Action offers can be an excellent way to make money online, but amid all of the legitimate opportunities, there exists some sites and companies which should be avoided.

Like any business, choosing which advertisers to pair with can be incredibly important and making sure that you avoid the scam-orientated offers is one of the most important ways in which you can keep your revenue high.

As with any industry, making poor choices when it comes to offers can denigrate your business; it can turn off potential readers/clickers and can cost you money and potential profits from alternative, legitimate cost per action offers. But choosing which offers to avoid is not that simple.

There is not always just one master list which you can consult and check companies and offers to ensure their legitimacy. Indeed, I choose to follow several simple steps in order to better acquaint myself with the offers involved, making sure that I keep my profits and my revenues high, as well as my site viewers happy, by subscribing to some simple rules. When considering new offers, check them against these potential warning flags.

They are not set in concrete and common sense and judgement is always advised, but it can never hurt to know too much.

Stick With What You Know

One of the best (and most obvious) ways in which you can avoid falling for bad offers is to stick to those that you know to be tried and tested. While it may seem like the most obvious thing in the world, offers which have either proved to be a hit or have made you money are an excellent reference point.

Therefore, when looking to branch out, consider alternatives or expansions for those that you know and trust. Forming good working relationships with a number of the better and more trustworthy companies can ensure that you will be able to have access to new and interesting chances, allowing you to make new money with fresh content that you can trust.

This also puts you in a better negotiating position when it comes to commission; rather than relying on untested and possibly untrustworthy sources, building a better relationship with those you trust is a fantastic way of never having to turn to possibly bad CPA offers.

Find Trustworthy Advice

For those who are just starting out in the CPA offers game, finding trustworthy offers can be difficult, while learning which offers to avoid can be even tougher. Thankfully, there are a number of communities, across a number of platforms which offer guidance and support for those just starting out.

When taking your first steps into the online marketing world, finding a knowledgeable and trustworthy community can be a tremendous boon. With the help of those who have walked down this familiar path before, you can quickly be told (without necessarily knowing) if a company is best avoiding.

In these instances, before you have a solid grasp of who and what to avoid, it might help to become and involved member of the community, allowing you to run potential offers past more experienced members.

This is a fantastic way to get started on the right foot, allowing you to refine your knowledge without making a cataclysmic mistake. I try to become involved with as many new starters as possible, thanks to my own experience starting out.

You should remember that when you become a roaring success: giving back to the community can help others in a similar position.

If It Looks Too Good...

Perhaps the most important rule relies on you having followed the previous two steps first. When you have set yourself up in online marketing, and made moves towards finding trustworthy clients, you can start to realise which rates are standard among the industry and get a rough idea of the amount of commission you should be earning per action.

As such, when an offer comes along which appears too good to be true, it probably is.

If a strange new company is offering a ridiculous rate or product, then – as you become more attuned to the industry – you can readily recognise that this might not be as legitimate as it wishes to appear.

Over time, this sense will become more and more refined, allowing you to determine which offers are best suited to you, especially when used in conjunction with the first two points.

Where Else Can You Promote CPA Offers?

Advertising CPA offers on your website or your blog is a great place to start.

I have been getting great results by sharing information about CPA offers on my own pages as well as through my email list but there are other methods that can be used to draw attention to CPA offers and generate responses from a wider audience.

Using Advertising Links

I have been using advertising links that lead directly to the CPA offer to reach out to a wider audience. I see using advertising links as a good way to reach out to Internet users who are interested in a specific offer rather than users who are always on the lookout for good deals.

Users who constantly hunt for good deals are likely to subscribe to my email list or to visit my site regularly but advertising links allow me to reach out to Internet users who are shopping for a specific product. I use many sites and PPC services to share advertising links. The sites or services I use entirely depend on the audience I am trying to reach out to.

I have actually been organizing my CPA offers into categories that reflect the kind of audience that would be interested in the advertising links so I can choose the best site or PPC service for my links.

Choosing the best sites or PPC services for each CPA offer has become easier as I am getting more experience and can learn from the results I get with each advertising link.

Free Links

Advertising my CPA offers for free is as simple as creating a link that will be seen by Internet users who are likely to be interested in the product or the offer I am promoting. I have built a strong network of bloggers and have become an active member on different message boards in order to share my free links.

Quality comes before quantity. I could create as many free links as I wanted, for instance by commenting on blog posts on topics related to the offer I want to share or by creating new discussion threads in different message boards related to the CPA offer.

However, these links would basically be spam. They will quickly be deleted by bloggers or moderators and will be ignored by the users I want to target.

Sharing Links On Other Blogs

Getting advertising links featured on other blogs was not easy at first. I had to contact several bloggers before I found a small ground of people who were interested.

I select the CPA offers I share with my network of bloggers carefully and make sure the offers are valuable to their audience. The bloggers who share my advertising links are happy to do so because it is a way for them to provide their audience with interesting content. I don't hesitate to return the favor by featuring some of their articles and sharing links to their content on my own blog.

Free Advertising Links On Message Boards

Sharing unsolicited links on a message board is usually seen as spam unless the links are valuable to the average user of the message board. I have been an active member on different couponing message boards for years.

I check these message boards on a weekly basis and share a few CPA offers with the other members because I know they will be interested. I encourage the users to give me some feedback on the offers I share to get a better idea of what kind of advertising links are valuable to this audience.

Paid Advertising Links

I have invested in paid advertising links several times and always got good results. I use paid advertising links for the best CPA offers I come across. Paid links are a great way to reach out to a very specific niche I will probably never need to target again.

I have found that the best PPC services charge a little more but they properly target the audience I want to reach out to. I have also bought advertising links on Facebook and got a good return on my investment. My advice is

to research different PPC services to find one
that delivers the results they promise.

Chapter 13: Landing Pages Vs. Direct Advertising

Here's the million dollar question, and it might really be a million dollar question once you get proficient at marketing CPA offers.

If you plan to pay for advertising, should your links point directly to the advertiser's sales page, or should you send visitors to your own website's landing page first? You can probably find almost as many opinions on this topic as you can find people who promote affiliate offers.

Pros And Cons Of Sending Visitors Directly To An Advertiser

It's always better to only have to get somebody to click once instead of twice.

If your advertisements on Facebook or Google send people directly to the advertiser, you don't have to go through the extra work of sending them there after they get to your page. That might seem like a great argument in favor of direct-linking.

Also, you are probably sending the visitor to a very focused sales page. That means that you held somebody's attention enough to get them to click your advertiser, and you don't have to worry about them getting distracted. You have a better chance of them buying something or filling out a lead form, and that mean's you should have a better chance to make some money.

But there are, alas, a couple of problems with this logic.

• You have to rely upon your advertising platform and affiliate stats, and you cannot gather these yourself. If the numbers do not match up, how do you diagnose the problem or the culprit?

• You don't get a second chance to sell something else or entice visitors to join your email subscriber list if you send visitors directly to your affiliate program either. If the program happens to make a sale, you might get paid. But if they don't make a sale, you have probably lost the visitor.

Advantages Of Routing Visitors Through A Landing Page

By now, you have probably figured out that I usually lean towards making my own landing page. Maybe I'm a little paranoid, but I like to keep my own statistics. I can track visitors on my own website, and if they are very different from the numbers that the advertising platform or affiliate program show me, I know that there is a problem somewhere.

But mostly, I guess I just believe in second chances. In my own experience, some percentage of people will perform the action that I need to make some money, but a greater percentage won't cooperate. Even if I have a great offer that converts at twenty percent, that still leaves eighty percent of my traffic who did not find that the offer was the thing they were looking for.

If you route visitors to a landing page on your own website, you have a chance to grab the rest of the folks who just aren't buying that offer today.

 Who knows why some people buy and some people don't? We sure don't.

• Maybe they will buy tomorrow, and that is a good reason to try to capture their emails on your subscription list or encourage them to bookmark your website.

• They could be looking into something for a friend, and you want them to pass your site link along to their friend, and you do not want them to pass on the advertiser's page because you might not get credit for the sale.

• Maybe they want to buy something that is slightly different, and you might have some other offers on your website that are more attractive.

The risk here is that you might offer so many alternatives that you will distract your visitors. But if you use your own website, you have a better chance to come up with the perfect mix of offers and opportunities that can help you earn the most money.

Yeah, I lean towards routing traffic through my own site. But many top marketers simply send customers directly from an advertisement trough their affiliate program linking code, and they do very well.

The right answer for you probably depends upon your product, the traffic, and your skills. You might test both methods to see which one produces the most money.

Chapter 13: Getting Started In Cpa

Marketing

When it comes to CPA marketing there is an abundance of legitimate providers and sources out there, in fact, each year the number of CPA opportunities available to you will double or even triple in numbers.

Unfortunately, as CPA's popularity spreads like wildfire online, the number of competitors seeking to be credited first for recruiting prospects to their offers will also continue to grow.

Thankfully, with this guide in hand you will be able to begin your journey fully equipped to launch a full scale CPA marketing campaign, where you will be given every tool and resource you need to establish yourself within these niche markets and begin to generate revenue right away.

But before you can begin making money with CPA programs, you must register and be approved for CPA based accounts. These networks serve as a middleman between you and advertisers who are interested in having you recruit new business and prospects on their behalf. These CPA companies generate money by earning a percentage of all of your income paid to them through each offer itself.

While there are hundreds of potential CPA companies to choose from, you will want to focus on the ones producing the best CPA opportunities, screening programs and paying out on time.

One of the biggest mistakes that CPA newcomers make is in getting involved in far too many CPA offers before learning the ropes and knowing what programs are converting best, and will allow them to maximize their income based on the time and effort they put into it.

Getting accepted into programs is often difficult because failing to provide adequate information on the application form, or not being prepared for the phone interview often associated with joining CPA networks. For starters, you should write down a list of companies that you intend to apply to, and read over their terms and website information so that you are familiar with what is expected as well as how they operate.

Many of the top CPA programs work along the same lines, but sometimes there are specific requirements, such as having an active website that is generating traffic or having a certain amount of experience in different fields, so you will want to be prepared prior to applying. To begin, I recommend signing up for an account at Copeac.com. I have had tremendous success with Copeac, and it's also one of the easiest companies to be approved for.

Visit www.Copeac.com and click on the Affiliate Section to proceed to the sign up form as shown below:

http://copeac.com/affiliates/signuppage.asp

On the application page, you will be asked for information regarding your company, address, and payment information as well as to verify your application by entering in your telephone number. When you apply with Copeac, they will verify your information by calling the phone number that you enter into the application form. This call is an automated one and you will be given a PIN code which you enter into the online application, so don't close this page until you have receive the call and entered in the unique code provided by the automated system. On most applications you will also be asked for your website details, including how much traffic your website is currently generating (if any), and whether you have experience in CPA marketing.

If you do not have a website, or your website is new, leave this field blank for now, but make sure that you enter in a statement into the comments area that indicates you do all of your marketing through Google Adwords or other Pay Per Click marketplaces.

Once you have completed the application, submit it for review.

The next step is to make the choice as to whether to give Copeac a few days to consider your application, or take the initiative to contact their offices and inform them that you have submitted an application and that you are interested in confirming receipt.

This will prompt the offices to verify you then and there (most of the time), giving you the opportunity to be accepted without having to wait for someone to review your online application.

When you are accepted, you will receive an acceptance form via email that will include your account details and additional information regarding the company. Be sure to read through the entire email and get acquainted with your assigned manager. He or she will be responsible for answering any questions you may have and following up with your progress.

Don't be afraid to ask for help! That's what they are there for, so if you have any concerns or are confused for any reason, shoot them off an email and get it squared away so you can move forward.

With many companies, your account manager will contact you by email or phone to introduce themselves and provide you with a bit of information about how the program works, how to set up your tracking properly and how to get started.

Best of all, after being accepted into a network such as Copeac, all future applications are easily approved by simply giving Copeac as a reference showing that you have already been screened and approved by a CPA based company.

Remember that with every application to a CPA company, your request will be manually reviewed and approved or rejected. This is not an automated process, so it can take a bit of time to have your accounts set up and ready to use. Unlike Copeac who welcomes newcomers, the majority of CPA companies will require that you have an online presence, meaning that you control or operate a website or blog, and that you have experience in online marketing. To get through their approval process, you will want to set up a blog or website and do a bit of work in generating traffic prior to applying for other CPA programs.

If you just don't want to do this however, there is a way around it that has worked for countless applicants who are new to CPA marketing or online business in general.

Here is how it's done:

•

When you fill out the application form, enter in a N/A where the website requirement field exists.

•

In the comments section of the application, indicate that you plan to promote CPA offers through PPC (Pay Per Click) marketing and that you have years of experience doing so.

•

Be prepared for a follow up phone call from these companies and when that happens, indicate that you have 2 years experience in PPC marketing.

-

If you are asked what offers you are interested in promoting, or if you hear the term "verticals", indicate to the representative that you are primarily interested in Entertainment, Business Opportunities, Health and Finance.

And finally, be sure to give accurate information about your location, including a valid email address. The last thing you want is to come all this way, be approved and then lose your account when they attempt to contact you via phone or email because you failed to keep your information up to date.

I strongly suggest that you set up a free gmail.com email account where it is accessible from anywhere, in the event you move.

Furthermore, with www.gmail.com, even if you have a website domain, you can forward emails to your gmail and reply from what appears to be your actual website domain (support@yourdomain.com) using the "Accounts" feature within the gmail account control panel.

Remember, most CPA companies are interested in seasoned marketers and experienced affiliates. They want to make as much money as possible through your efforts and will always give higher priority to those who are actively promoting offers and yielding results so be sure to indicate your experience in the applications comments fields and on the phone when asked.

If you are interested in maintaining your privacy, you could consider signing up for a toll free or local number with www.GotVMail.com . They offer affordable monthly plans and provide accounts with full features, including call forwarding, call screening and call masking, that provides privacy while ensuring that you are able to be reached whenever needed.

If you miss a telephone call from a CPA company looking to talk to you about your application, be sure to phone them back at your earliest convenience. Don't wait for them to contact you again!

Take initiative to call them to complete your application. This shows them that you are genuinely interested in their company and in working with them.

Other CPA Companies:

www.Advaliant.com

Performance based company providing online advertisers with high performing lead generation, traffic sources and transactional programs that maximize ROI. Advaliant offers high margins and optimal site profitability.

Hydra Network www.hydranetwork.com

This is a very popular CPA company who boasts that they will beat any payout from any program running the same campaign. Hydra is exceptional at ensuring prompt payouts and offering reliable customer support. I've done very well with their offers and in many cases; their programs are unique and exclusive to their network.

Never Blue

http://www.neverblue.com/index.html

Neverblue is a premier global performance-based affiliate network that brings together choice affiliates and quality online advertisers as partners through carefully monitored, custom advertising. Our affiliates use a combination of different marketing tactics, including search engine marketing, email marketing, contextual advertising, incentive marketing and banner ads.

Max Bounty

http://www.maxbounty.com

Affiliates with MaxBounty earn revenue from advertising sponsors on a pay-for-performance basis. We have both in-house managed campaigns for you to advertise, and merchants wanting direct relationships with you.

ROI Rocket

http://www.roirocket.com/

ROI Rocket offers:

Targeted campaigns specific to YOUR Marketing needs High Payouts on Performance Based Ad Campaigns Competitive, timely Payouts

Exclusive Destination Specific Offers Tailored

Highly Responsive Full Service Account Management Team

Market Leverage https://marketleverage.com

It's simple...MarketLeverage Publishers enjoy higher payouts on hundreds of different advertisements while getting the best customer service in the performance marketing industry. Our experienced team of Publisher managers are trained to help our Publishers earn more money from their website, search engine and email marketing efforts.

CPA Empire

http://www.cpaempire.com

CPA Storm

http://www.cpastorm.com

« Absolute best pricing available

« Flexible payment options

« Dedicated customer support

« Premium Fortune 1000 advertisers

« Accurate real time reporting and tracking

« Every offer tested for performance

« Custom creative and offers

« Newsletters to fit your audience

« No cost to join

Rocket Profit https://www.rocketprofit.com

No-risk exposure to huge a publisher base

Detailed, state of the art tracking capability

Ability to help generate fresh performing creative

Unsurpassed customer support - phone, email, IM

NO FEES to get your offers on our affiliate network

100% Performance Based Advertising Vehicle

Proven Track Record of Successful campaigns

Blue Phoenix Network
https://www.bluephoenixnetwork.com/

Real Time statistics and Reporting

Prompt payouts

Quality campaigns to promote

Top-tier advertisers and exclusives!

Aquasis Media
https://partners.aquasismedia.com

IncentaClick

http://www.incentaclick.com/

CX Digital Media is committed to generating revenue for our affiliates! Our Famous 7 day ROI guarantee does not just apply to advertisers. We are confident that your inventory will convert better than it could through any other affiliate network.

Revenue Loop

http://www.revenueloop.com

RevenueLoop provides publishers access to thousands of online advertisers. All offers are tracked by a real-time, online accounting system, giving our publishers complete control over their campaign.

aZoogleAds https://www.azoogleads.com

AzoogleAds is a performance-based online advertising network that delivers both amazing results for its Advertisers and easy to manage and highly profitable revenue stream for its Publishers.

Rextopia

http://rextopia.com/

Choosing Your Offers

With each program, you are going to be given a variety of options for promoting and earning based on the current offers that are available.

From ring tones, education, entertainment, home business, email/zip submits, downloads and trial accounts right down to financial/debt offers, dating and relationships and even work from home there is no shortage of offers to choose to promote.

The problem is that you want to maximize your time and earnings, and even the most avid marketer isn't able to cover every program out there, so you'll need to chisel down into the available opportunities and choose the hottest programs that will convert.

One of the tools that will help you weed through offers to find out which ones are likely to convert better is the Aff Spy tool available at www.AffSpy.com and the second, available at www.OfferVault.com

These two resources will provide you with information regarding offer viability, payout information and popularity as well as additional information based on overall network payouts from some of the top offers out there.

You can explore additional CPA offers and networks by reviewing the extensive directory located at: http://www.affiliateseeking.com/ netwo/23000002/1.html

Before choosing an offer to promote however, you will want to do a bit of keyword research. Choosing the right keywords is essential if you are planning to promote CPA offers with pay per click (PPC) marketing on service sites like Google Adwords because essentially, if you fail to create a relevant keyword swipe file, you will end up paying a fortune in clicks to your advertisements that don't produce results.

To begin, visit https://adwords.google.com/select/Keyword ToolExternal

You will want to choose an offer to investigate first, so that you can come up with keywords relating to that offer.

Here is an example:

With this offer, the payout is $1.75 for each person that fills in the contest form. Initially, looking at this offer a few target groups come to mind, such as university students, high school graduates who will go off to university soon, and so on.

Some of the keywords that would target this offer would be:

- college scholarship cash

- free college scholarship

- college scholarship money

- college scholarship help

and so on.

After entering in these keywords into the Google Keyword tool, I yielded over 97 results, these are potential keywords that are currently entered into the Google search engine by people seeking out information similar in nature..

- help me pay for college

- how to pay for college

- grants to pay for college

- help with paying for college

- ways to pay for college

- and so on.

You will need to go through the keyword list, choosing the phrases that you believe would be as targeted as possible to the offer, and add them to your keyword swipe file.

The next step is to assign these keywords into specific groups for your Google advertisements. Most people will focus on long tail keyword phrases, these are longer phrases rather than primary keywords which would be far more competitive and harder to rank for. To create your ad groups, simply enter in each of your selected keywords from the initial listing that Google provided you with. For instance, if I entered in "ways to pay for college", the Google keyword tool would generate keyword phrases like:

- creative ways to pay for college

-

the best way to pay for college

-

alternative ways to pay for college

and so on. These keywords will provide you with the ability to set up specific ad groups in Google Adwords,

When running PPC ads for CPA offers, you want to ensure that you pre-qualify your traffic; otherwise you will end up paying for clicks to your ads that amount to nothing. In order to do this, I suggest including the required action in your advertisement. For example, if your CPA offer requires an email address, include that within your Google Advertisement such as "Enter in your email address for your chance to win".

Doing this will lower your cost and ensure that your advertisements are far more targeted. You will also want to register a domain name that includes your primary keyword, if possible. In our example above, registering a domain such as collegeforfree.com or freecollegegrants would be two great domains for promoting this offer.

Once you have your domain name and your advertisement groups and ads set up, you will want to ensure that you redirect your ad through your domain name to your CPA offer.

Sound confusing? It's really easy. You simply register your domain name and forward it to your CPA referral link, direct to the publisher.

This means that when someone clicks on your advertisement, they will be sent to your domain name, which instantly switches, and transfers them to the CPA offers landing page.

Recap:

•

Select a handful of CPA offers from network sites.

•

Run keywords into Google's External tool to create a keyword swipe file.

•

Run those keywords through Google's External tool to create ad groups.

•

Set up your Google advertisement campaigns using these keywords.

-

Include the 'call to action' within your advertisements to pre-screen visitors.

If you are not familiar with Google Adwords, you should read through their help center prior to setting up a campaign or running an advertisement.

You can find additional information here:

http://www.google.com/adwords/learningcenter/

Digital Point also offers a free keyword research tool as well available at: http://www.digitalpoint.com/tools/suggestion/

With PPC marketing, you will want to stay on top of your advertisements and how well they are converting. Since you are paying for every single click, you will want to make sure that your ads are working well, and from time to time, tweaking might be required, and in some cases removing ad groups entirely if they just aren't producing results.

Choosing Your Model

When you join CPA networks, you will often be given the opportunity to choose between a CPA or Revenue Share model.

With CPA, since you are paid one lump sum for each completed action, you must consistently work at generating new leads and prospects.

For example, if you are promoting a gambling website, such as a poker gaming company, you may be paid out each time someone you refer to the poker website signs up for a free account or takes advantage of a free trial offer.

Once that prospect has completed the required action, and you are paid accordingly, you will no longer earn money from that particular person and must go on to recruit and refer others in order to continue to receive payment. With Revenue Share, you are offered a percentage or an ongoing payment plan for each prospects activities. In the example of a poker website, if you referred a user who joined the website you may be paid out a percentage of their account funding when playing the games, or a flat rate for specific amounts that your prospects spend while a member of these websites.

When you are new to CPA offers, choosing whether to join the CPA offer or the Revenue Share model can be a difficult decision to make.

Many new CPA affiliates typically go with the CPA offers because they are unable to effectively gauge how valuable each referred prospect may be, and how much more money they are given the opportunity of earning from each person rather than consistently scouting our new referrals.

Personally, I prefer to go with the Revenue Share model as often as possible so that I am able to work smarter, not harder, as with the RS campaigns, I am able to focus on recruiting a specific number of active participants and continuing to profit from their ongoing activities.

If you are unsure what will work best for you, start off by promoting a handful of CPA programs, and accept an equal number of Revenue Share offers. Then, spend a couple of months promoting both equally and determine which ones are yielding better results.

From that information collected, you will be able to focus primarily on the ones that generate maximum profits while weeding out any inactive or poorly converting campaigns that you are struggling to profit from. Being successful with CPA or related marketing campaigns often takes time, and only through personal experience can you really determine what programs will produce the best results for you, so spend some time thoroughly evaluating a handful of potentially profitable programs and see what you can do!

PPC Marketing Starter Guide

With it comes to CPA marketing, as mentioned in a previous chapter, PPC (Pay Per Click) marketing is one of the most popular methods of jump-starting your campaign and making money with fresh programs or new opportunities.

To help you get started, I have devoted an entire chapter to PPC marketing that will show you exactly how to set up your accounts and campaigns.

As you begin your CPA journey, another important tool of the trade is in setting up your Google Adwords PPC account, so that you can begin to promote your CPA offers. You can create your account by visiting: http://adwords.google.com/select/Login Click on Start Now to begin the registration process.

The next page will offer you the ability to create either a Starter Account or a Standard Edition.

Keyword Targeting allows Adwords advertisers to select keywords that when typed into Googles' search engine by visitors will instantly trigger your ads to appear within the Sponsored Listings area as well as within other areas of the Google Network.

Placement Targeting allows advertisers to choose specific websites that they would like their advertisements to appear on. You can choose to show your ads on specific pages within these websites or select site-wide targeting which would display your as on various pages of the websites you target.

Select Standard Edition and click "Continue".

In order to continue, you will need a Google account. This can include a gmail account, Orkut or even iGoogle.

If you do not currently have a Google based account, select "I do not use these other services" to be given additional options, such as using your domain based email account or perhaps the one provided to you by your Internet Service Provider.

If you already use services such as Gmail or Igoogle, click the first option, "I have an email address and password from within the Google network".

A drop down box will appear with additional options. Select "I'd like to use my existing Google account for Adwords", unless you are interested in setting up a new gmail account exclusively for your Adwords campaigns.

Upon completion, you will reach an account registration thank you page that indicates you must confirm your request by checking your email and clicking on the validation link contained in your introductory welcome email.

If you do not see this email in your inbox, be sure to check your spam folder as sometimes emails sent out this way, may end up filtered there.

Once you have verified your request, you will be able to log into your Google Adwords account and set up your campaigns. Google will also ask for information concerning your target audience including whether you wish to focus on specific groups by language or location.

Typically, I choose English and include countries like Canada, United States, UK, and Australia, however you can easily edit your targeted locations at any time should you wish to make changes to the groups of people that will be able to see your ads later on.

The flexibility offered through language and location targeting allows advertisers to develop content tailored to specific groups, nationalities and locations. This is an exceptional benefit of the Adwords system if you are planning to cater to specific languages such as French or Spanish, or you are interested in only having your advertisements appear to residents of certain countries.In order to completely activate your account, you will have to enter in your billing information. You can do this at a later date, once you have set up your campaigns and are ready to launch them. You will also be required to pay a one-time activation fee.

Once you have activated your account and set up your campaigns, you will begin to see your advertisements appear within minutes, however if you are advertising on Googles partner websites, all ads must be reviewed to ensure that they follow the guidelines, prior to being displayed within the network.

To get started, log into your Adwords campaign and click on the "Campaign Management" tab at the top. When you create campaigns, you will design each one so that it's focused on specific groups. In order to do that, you will enter in keyword phrases associated to the markets that you advertise to.

Look for the area titled "Active Campaigns". Within that area you will see a drop-down menu that includes "Create Online Campaign". That is where you go create your first Adwords campaign.

Once inside that area, you will be given the opportunity to create a keyword-targeted campaign or a Placement-Targeted campaign.

With keyword targeted campaigns your ads will target specific keyword groups and when those are entered into the search engine, your ads will be triggered to appear. With Placement-Targeted campaigns, your advertisements will be featured on specific websites in Google's content network.

For now, let's go with "Keyword Targeted" campaign.

On the next page, you will need to enter in a Campaign title and to name your new ad group. Be sure to select a campaign title that you will easily recognize later on, when you have multiple campaigns within your Adwords account. It will save you a lot of time if you set this up correctly, right from the start.

You will always be required to assign one ad group to each campaign but can assign multiple ad groups as well, if you wish.

Ad groups allow you to target specific groups of keywords, and I recommend including only 5-8 keywords per group.

You will also have to choose your language based targeting options and in the event you wish to advertise to multiple language groups, you can hold down your CTRL key (on a PC) or Command key (on a Mac) to select more than one language group. I choose English when I set up my campaigns because that is the primary language of my website.

You will also have to choose the locations that you wish to advertise to. By default, the country in which you are located will be chosen but you can select other countries from the list by clicking on "Change Targeting".

To get started, enter in the name of the country that you are looking to add to your campaign, and check the box next to the country name in order to successfully move it over to your location listing.

Each time you check a location (next to the country name), it will be added to your listing, as shown below:

You are also able to select location bundles which can save you time as these are areas grouped together by Google Adwords such as "United States and Canada" or "North America Bundle".

If you were interested in promoting your campaigns to multiple countries, you can select as many of these bundles as you wish and move them into your advertising campaign. Once you have set up the locations, click "DONE" to complete the process. You will now be returned to your previous location which will show you a splash page indicating all of the countries that you have selected. Confirm that these are accurate, and click Continue to proceed to the next step.

This part of the process is an exceptionally important one - creating your campaigns advertisement (ad copy).

In fact, this is the most important aspect of your Adwords marketing because if your ad is not set up to attract attention, convert viewers into clicks / visitors and filter out freebie seekers and those who are not likely going to buy from you, it can end up costing you a lot of money in worthless clicks and significantly decrease your quality score.

You will also need to enter in specific keywords. Initially, you should focus on targeting 2-5 keywords per ad and ensure that each keyword is highly relevant to your advertisement, and that all keywords contained within your ad group are all related (focused on the same advertisement).

You will then need to set your daily budget, as well as your maximum bid per click. I suggest setting your daily budget to $25.00 when you first start out, and your maximum bid per click at $.25.

If you set either of these too high, you will end up in "Google debt", especially if you are new to Adwords and are just learning how the system works as well as how to create high converting campaigns.

This is also where most new marketers end up making the biggest mistake of their PPC activities, by setting a daily budget and/or a maximum bid far above what they can really afford, so be careful to start off slow and increase your budget as you become experienced with Adwords.

Another great benefit of using Google is that they place no minimum order restrictions on accounts. This means that you can start advertising on Google without having to invest a lot of money. In addition, you can easily edit your budget at any time should you wish to start off small and increase it as you become more experienced using the system.

Remember, you are not charged each time your ad appears within Google's Sponsored Listings, and instead, are only charged each time someone clicks on your ad and is directed to whatever website you have associated with that particular campaign.

The amount you will pay for every click on your ad will be dependant on many things, including how much you intend to bid for exposure.

For example, if you set a maximum bid as $.20 and I set my maximum bid at $.10, your ad will appear higher than mine within the Sponsored Advertiser column. However, when someone clicks on your ad you will end up paying more than I will for clicks to mine.

This means that you have to figure out what the best placement is in order to maximize your advertising costs.

Some people have studied Adwords placement versus clicks and have determined that being the top sponsor doesn't always yield better results.

In fact, there are many expert Adwords users that claim that being the second, third and even fourth placed ad will generate more exposure and end up costing you less for every visitor to your website.

If you enter in $20.00 as your daily budget, and are paying $.10 per click, you will receive about 200 clicks before your daily budget has been reached. Once it is reached, your ads will no longer appear within the Sponsored Categories until the next day when your daily budget is reset.

Within your Adwords account, you are able to create as many campaigns as you wish.

Each campaign typically focuses on individual CPA promotions. For instance, if I were involved in two different programs, such as Ring Tones and Online Dating, I would set up two different campaigns using keywords and ad copy specific to those markets. As a Google Adwords advertiser, you should always stay on top of how your campaigns are performing.

The best way to do this is to label your campaigns based on something you will easily recognize. If you end up creating dozens of campaigns, you will want to call them something that makes it simply for you to recognize as soon as you log into your account.

After creating your campaigns, you will need to assign keywords to each one. These are called "Ad Groups" and they consist of keyword phrases that are relevant to your products.

Google Adwords Quality Score Explained

Google advertisers are familiar with what is known as the "Quality Score" and there is good reason for this. Your quality score will directly affect the amount you are required to pay for each click to your site. The higher your quality score is, the lower your cost per click will be.

Furthermore, if you focus on obtaining a high quality score, not only will your campaigns be more affordable BUT you will receive the same exposure as you were when you were paying more per click!

The reason why Google implemented a quality score into their PPC marketplace was partly due to quality control.

They knew that by integrating a system in which advertisers were rated based on their campaigns performance, they would essentially cut back on bogus campaigns and irrelevant keywords and advertisements from being featured.

Since the quality score is based on your CTR (Click Through Rate), advertisers want their campaigns to convert into clicks as often as possible whenever they are featured throughout the PPC marketplace.

Besides, as a PPC marketer, even if the quality score didn't exist you still want to ensure that those who are viewing your ads clearly understand what it is that you are offering, because since you are paying for each click to your site, there is no sense in yielding visitors who have little or no interest in your product.

This is why it's important to focus on creating targeted campaigns that combine relevant keywords with solid ad-content, such as a compelling title, descriptive ad body, and a high converting landing page.

Every element of a PPC campaign is an important one that ties everything together.

If one aspect of your campaign is lacking, it can dramatically impact your results, which is why so many people experience failure when initially promoting through PPC marketplaces.

They throw their campaigns together, compile huge listings of irrelevant keywords, and create advertisements that attract freebie seekers rather than pre-selling prospects and targeting only potential buyers, not visitors.

Another thing to keep in mind when striving for a high quality score is that sites like Google retain information regarding your PPC marketing history.

This means that even if you pause or remove an ineffective campaign, it can directly affect your quality score so it's very important to focus on creating effective campaigns right from the start.

On a final note, when you initially create campaigns within Google Adwords, you will be given an estimated CTR for each campaign.

This will occur whenever you assign a new keyword to your campaigns as well, and can you quickly determine whether a specific keyword phrase is likely to perform well or not. While this is a general guideline and is not always accurate, it can help you eliminate keyword phrases that are not going to convert.

There are many different ways that I personally use Adwords to promote CPA offers. First, I use Keyword Targeted Campaigns on Google Search itself, as well as Keyword Targeted Campaigns within the content network and finally, Placement Targeted campaigns specifically for websites and positioning on website pages that feature Google Adsense advertising.

This means that I can select specific websites in which I want my CPA advertising to appear AND can choose the ad blocks that I wish to occupy.

After you have determine that CPA offers you intend to promote, the next step is to log into your CPA account to obtain information relating to your offer. In our example, I will use NeverBlueAds as my CPA network of choice. Simply register your account at: https://secure.neverblue.com/signup/

Once inside, click on the "Campaigns" tab to browse through the variety of offers available. You can also click on "Top Search Campaigns" to view the most popular offers currently available.

These offers are also the top performing offers, so it's important to focus your attention on this data in order to choose the offers that are more likely going to generate a higher payout.

In order to develop the ability to choose high paying, high converting offers, you will need to develop and fine tune your keyword research skills as well as be able to create marketing strategies directed at each of the offers you choose.

For email submit offers, where you are paid for every valid and unique email address that one of your website visitors enter into a merchants form, you can expect to be paid anywhere from $1.00 up to $2.00 each.

NeverBlue offers some of the best email-submit based offers so it's wise to browse through their current programs and choose one to start. Email submits are by far the easiest CPA offers to earn with, if you are able to develop a website or well crafted landing page.

Once you have selected your offers, you will need to develop a keyword list using Googles Keyword External Search Tool at:

https://adwords.google.com/select/Keyword ToolExternal

You will want to choose very targeted keywords and keyword phrases otherwise you will end up spending far more money in Pay Per Click marketing than you will want to, so be sure to weed through the list of keywords and focus only on the ones that you believe will convert the best.

Of course, you will want to keep a close eye on your performance, tweaking your campaigns, and removing keywords that just aren't working.

Using Polls With CPA Offers

One of the methods that savvy CPA marketers use to increase conversions and promote their CPA offers, is to integrate polls into their website pages. While many marketers will claim that this technique no longer works, I am here to tell you that it absolutely, 100% does work and it works extremely well.

Here is how I do it:

I set up a new poll every week so that the content is fresh and return visitors are given the chance to continue to participate. Each time I set up a new poll, I focus it on a specific CPA offer.

Polls work best with email/zip submits where you are paid for each unique entry made by your website visitors. I then create a poll that asks a simple question pertaining to my CPA offer.

For example, if I were promoting an iPod CPA offer, I would set up a poll to ask:

Do You Have An iPhone?

Yes - No

Enter your email address for a chance at receiving a FREE iPhone!

Visitors would then choose yes, or no and enter in their email address. I would receive credit for their email submit and the form/poll would direct them to the CPA network website.

Using Sub ID's For Tracking

In order to keep on top of your efforts you will want to properly track your conversions, which is especially important if using PPC marketing to promote your CPA offers, as each click will cost you and you'll want to ensure that your advertisements are converting and your costs are justified.

One easy way of detecting what keywords are performing well within your PPC campaigns is to utilize the sub ID option available through CPA networks.

Sub-ID Tracking is the process in which an affiliate passes data to CPA networks such as

MaxBounty in a click that can be returned back to the affiliate if/when a lead is generated from that click. MaxBounty currently supports the tracking of up to two pieces of sub-ID data.

Passing in Sub-ID Data

To enable sub-ID tracking, you need to add at least one sub-ID parameter to any tracking link you get from MaxBounty.

These parameters are called s1 and s2. The s1 parameter is used for basic sub-ID tracking and the s2 is used for more advanced sub-ID tracking.

Examples

If you were advertising a "Win a TV" campaign on your site, MaxBounty would give you a tracking link like this:

http://www.mb01.com/lnk.asp?o=26&c=233&a=1000

Example 1 - If you wanted to keep track of any of your members who generated a "Win a TV" lead for you, you could put their e-mail addresses in the s1 parameter, like this:

http://www.mb01.com/lnk.asp?
o=26&c=233&a=1000&s1=submember@mysi
te.com

Example 2 - If you wanted to keep track of any of your own affiliates who generated a lead for you, and you also wanted to keep track of how much you'd be paying them, you could put their sub-affiliate ID in the s1 parameter and the rate you'd be paying them in the s2 parameter, like this:

http://www.mb01.com/lnk.asp?
o=26&c=233&a=1000&s1=4531&s2=0.40

NOTE: MaxBounty provides a tool that allows you to easily populate the s1 parameter when you grab your links from the system. By attaching this to your tracking URL's that you are given by the CPA networks, you are able to see whenever a specific advertisement has yielded results via an action taken by a prospect, as well as how many clicks each tracking Url has received and how well it is converting into commission based actions.

Tie this in with Google Adwords option to include the variable [Keyword that you can use on your landing page, you will be able to keep on top of all active advertisements in your PPC campaigns.

Chapter 14: Finding Good Cpa Offers

Before you get started, make sure you select 3-6 CPA offers to promote. Usually Lead Generation/ Cost Per Lead/ Pay Per Lead

/ Email or Zip submit offers does best for me.

Usually I chose a country that has an English speaking population or English is one of its official languages.

This will help:

https://en.wikipedia.org/wiki/List_of_territori al_entities_wher
e_English_is_an_official_language

If you're looking to target them in their local language, then you

can do it. Just go to Fiverr and get your ads and pages translated to the language you want.

Coming to the offers, less number of fields you offer is easier to make it convert. Like the below offer has just 4 fields – first name, last name, contact no. and email. Once anyone fills that In I get paid.

What niche?

More related to your niche the better, but instead of selecting offers based on just your niche think broad.

E.g. If you targeting women in the age group 21-25 for a hair loss offer, then think what other things she would be interested in. Maybe weight loss offers as she wants to look good. Free coupons/ deals, make money. You can promote them anything

if you find the right angle to promote it to them.

You'll see how I do this in my next section (Thank you page)

Also note the requirement of your CPA offers, like what kind of promotional methods they allow, age group, countries,

conversion point, mobile optimized – this will play an

important role while targeting.

Why?

Because, if you have selected a CPA offer that pays you just for leads in the age group of 21-25 years and you might be running ads for 24-30 years, so you might lose a lot of commissions there (I made this mistake twice).

Also, check if the offers you are promoting are mobile optimized or not. If they are, you can test both mobile ads and desktop ads to them. In my experience, if your CPA offers are mobile optimized they convert well with Facebook traffic.

I hope you are getting my point.

Module 2 – Creating your Giveaway

This is Step 1 of our method. Before we create our giveaway we need to find a physical product that resonates with people we are targeting.

You can even do a digital product, but from my experience physical products do the best.

There are 2 ways to do it.

1) Find a passionate niche & create/find a unique product around that niche.

e.g. - German shepherd lovers & create a tee shirt that they can wear and feel proud of.

You can look at different tee designs that sold well on Teespring, create a similar design and put it away for giveaway (after they opt in - say if they can't wait to get it, they can directly buy it right away)

Find tees from Sunfrogshirts.com, they have no minimums, you can be an affiliate for any tee-shirt you

want to sell and get paid for every tee-shirt you make a

sale for.

2) Pick an already established brand and create a giveaway around their product.

Piggyback on big brands. Go to amazon or any other shopping site, look for a product that is mid-priced of a popular brand. I usually look for products between $30-

$60.

Look for something that people really need or like. Put yourself in their shoes. Ask friends, family etc. It's easy.

Like if you're in gaming niche, chose an upcoming/newly released game.

Make up kits works well if you are in beauty niche. Weight loss niche – protein powders, shakes etc.

I like to go with the 2ND method since it's easier. Here is one of the product I selected for one of my giveaways.

It's a Philip's Miss Freshers hair styling kit that I found on this local

shopping site. So when I announce the results, I just ask the winner for their address. Go to the site, make an order, put the winners address and name in and that's it.

Module 3 – Building your machine

Once you have selected the product you want to giveaway, we need to setup few things before we get started.

Step1) Create your Facebook fan page

Go here and create a fan page https://www.facebook.com/pages/create

Choose Brand or Website, choose your category. Choose a name according to the niche you are in.

For e.g. if you are in cooking niche, name it as I LOVE Cooking, Cooking Club, Kitchen Corner

If you're in beauty niche, Beauty Queens, Beauty Tips for Her.

Other examples in dog niche - German Shepherd Lovers, Pitbull

Lovers ect etc.

Upload a profile image and a cover pic. Make 3-4 posts on

your page and you're ready to go.

Step 2) Build your landing pages

You don't need a very fancy landing page, simple works the best. I always get between 50-70% opt in rates depending on the offer.

Here is how my landing page looks for the 'Philips Miss

Fresher's Styling Kit' product...

I use Instabuilder 2.0 to create my opt-in page and thank you page. Even if you don't have Instabuilder 2.0, you can use any page builder or editor. You just need to make sure you have these 6 important elements on your page

1) A Big Headline about What They Will Win

2) Product/Giveaway Image

3) How to enter the contest

4) Call to action (Opt-in form)

5) How winners will be selected (many people ask, so just mention how you are going to select the winners, I use Woobox App)

6) Privacy Policy and Terms of use Page (If you don't have

those, Facebook might reject your ads)

Next is to create your Thank You Page. Again I use Instabuilder

2.0 for this, but I like I said you can use any page builder you have.

Make sure you have these 5 elements in your thank you page.

1) Congratulate them, tell them their email is verified

2) Tell them to check their email in 10 min (I will tell you why to do this in a short while)

3) Ask them to complete the offers you listed below to increase their chances of winning

4) List 3-4 CPA offers (Pay per Lead) below. (I make sure they are paying me at least $0.35) When they check their email in 10 min, they

will again have the option to complete the offers below and increase their chances of winning.

5) Thank you

Step 3) Setting up your Auto-responder / welcome email /

promo emails

In the very first email I send to them, I just thank them for participating. Tell them about how and when the winners will be selected.

I make sure I have these 2 things in my very first welcome email

to them:

1) From field – Your Name (Fanpage name)

2) Subject – *Contest name+ Important details...

What to actually write in your first email/welcome email?

Have a look at the exact email I send them once they sign up for the contest:

1) Congratulations and Thanks

2) Introduce who you are and tell them you run the Facebook page (name)

3) When you'll be announcing the winners

4) Again, just like in the thank you page, tell them if they want to increase their chances of winning, complete the CPA offers below.

Use the exact template I told you above and you'll do well.

What to write in your follow up emails?

An email list is your asset, treat it right and you will make more money and for a long time.

Starting 2nd day, you can follow the template below

Here is what you do:

Day 1) Send them some tips/value email

Day 2) Send them another value email + soft presell for an offer

Day 3) Promote the offer

Day 4) Remind them about the offer + Benefits

Day 5) FAQ's about the offer

Day 6) Scarcity – LAST CHANCE email

Then repeat the same sequence for other CPA offer or any offer

you want to promote.

Other ways to monetize your list:

Build a viral blog in your niche, put Adsense, CPA offers, use Content advertising sites like

Taboola, Outbrain to monetize your traffic. (Also add Facebook share and like button on your posts)

Create a viral video blog, add funny videos, tips videos from Youtube and put them in your blog, monetize it Adsense, CPA offers, Banner ads, Content advertising sites as Taboola, Outbrain. (Also add Facebook share and like button on your posts)

People love to like and share viral stuff.

Mail regularly to your list, also post the viral stuff on your fan page. People love to like and share such stuff.

Module 4 – Launching Your Ads

Unlike in any other course or methods, you need not be an expert in writing your ad copy or in creating your ad image.

Step 1) Post about the contest on your Fan page

I learned this while doing Teespring.

I just ask them a simple question first such as – Love your hair? Love cooking? Love reading? And then – add win a FREE "XYZ"!

Again I keep it simple and it works for me each and every time. Go to your Facebook fan page, post a picture and add few lines:

1) Ask them a simple question.

2) Tell them what they will win FREE

3) Like your post/page

4) Enter here: Your landing page link

5) Giveaway/product image (just add a border around it and add Win FREE at the top before posting)

That's it. Easy.

Don't ask them to share your post as Facebook don't allow it and they will reject your ad.

Step 2) Find your target audience

This is one of the most important steps you need take care of. Get this wrong and you will not reach your target audience, lower CTR, higher Cost Per Click, Cost Per Lead and you make less money.

This is not difficult I will show you how to do it correctly.

Before even starting your ad, you need to find your audience, what are their demographics, age, sex, what they buy, where they hang out, education, do these guys have money or not.

How to find that,

1) Alexa.com – Find a popular website in your niche, go to alexa and type in the name, go to bottom and check.

2) Audience Insight (Facebook) – Go inside your FB ads, find

audience insight, in interest type your competitors, big brands, big names, websites in your niche. You can find a lot of data about your demographics there.

Once you know your demographics, you can also think of various related offers you can promote to them.

Whom to target?

I get this question tons of times about whom to target. They have the offer, they got the ads created, but they are not sure about whom to target.

Here is a list that will be helpful

1) Celebrities in the niche

2) Books, Authors

3) Websites, Forums, Blogs

4) Products, Brands

5) Associations, clubs, events

Use Audience Insight – Page Categories and Affinity Score (higher better, over 10X is good). Click on those links and see if they are related and add them to your interests. Repeat the same with each new interest.

The above are all related to Indian Beauty and Fashion niches. Add

more interests from make-up brands to get more ideas.

Below is an example for affinity when I added Ryan Diess, Frank Kern as interest. Sometimes you might not find a lot of related terms with high affinity. Keep trying different interests.

Now create a list of 15-20 interests you found to use for targeting in the next step.

For the "Styling Kit" offer I found 5 interests, Lakme, Oriflame, Mac, Loreal and Revlon (enough to start with)
Setup your conversion pixel

One thing I forgot to mention above is Conversion Pixel, it lets you track the no. of leads you generate for each ad. This helps in removing/pausing the bad performing ads from the good

ones.

Go   here: https://www.facebook.com/ads/manage/con vtrack/

Choose Create Pixel. On the next step, select leads, name the conversion pixel

Click on view Pixel code, copy the code that's generated:

Next is copy the code, and put between the <head> </head>

section on your Thank You Page (every person reaching your thank you page – means they have opted in – are tracked as leads.)

Visit your thank you page once and conversion pixel will be activated.

Step 3) Creating your ads (NO ONE IS TEACHING THIS)

Ok guys, you will not find this anywhere. I have been testing this method for some time now and I realized it's giving me better results than any of my other Facebook ad methods.

You might have seen other people running Tee-shirt ads or contest ads, they say to run PPE (Pay Per Engagement/Boosted Ads) ads thru Ad-Manager.

PPE ads vs Website Conversion ads

I have tried that, they work fine. They give you tons of likes and shares, but our main aim here is to get maximum people to opt- in so we can make CPA commissions on our Thank you page

and then promoting them more stuff through email.

And that's why website conversion ads works the best,

Facebook optimize our ads for maximum conversions to get the best results. Also it's easier to track and optimize them.

But there was a big PROBLEM!

You cannot run POST ads with Website Conversion with Ads
Manager.

So we found a way to do it with Power Editor. ;) Here is the link to it: https://www.facebook.com/ads/manage/po wereditor/

The first thing you need to do after you open Power Editor, make sure:

1) Click on the "Download to Power Editor" button and

download all your Facebook Ads Manager data

2) Make sure "Manage Ads" option is selected on the left

Of your screen.

How Power Editor works?

Step 1) Create a new campaign

Step 2) Create new Ad set (link to the campaign) Step 3) Create new Ads (link to the ad set)

Step 4) Upload and save changes.

Don't worry, I will take you each step slowly so you understand it properly. Make sure you observe it carefully and when you create your ads inside the power editor. Keep this guide open for help. □

Step 1) Create a new campaign

Ok, before we start we need to see the list of interests we prepared during our research. I am going to use "Tresemme" as an interest for this example. I found it on the local ecommerce site in the hair care section.

The next step is to create your campaign inside the Power

Editor.

1) Click on the + button under the campaigns section

2) Name your new campaign

3) Name your new ad set – name it as – campaign + interest

4) Select the conversion pixel to track leads

Click create

Step 2) Create new Ad set (link to the campaign)

Now you'll be inside your new Ad Set

 (Complete the below steps first and then select the budget at

last after editing your audience)

Use the table below while selecting budget for your ads

Audience: 500,000 – 1,300,000 - $5 daily budget

1,300,001 – 1,500,000 - $7 daily budget

1,500,001 – 1,750,000 - $9 daily budget

Scroll down, remove everything except "Desktop News Feed"

Make sure Optimization & Pricing should look like this.

Here is where we edit our audience

On the next page, you need to edit your audience

1) Enter country/countries you targeting

2) Enter age group (my ideal audience was 21-26, but the audience size was just 230,000 so I added more interests)

3) Enter sex you are targeting

4) Exclude people who have already liked your page

5) Enter your interests (If you audience size is already above

500,000 well and good. If not, then add more interest to make it at least 500,000)

Click on Save

Step 3) Create new Ads (link to the ad set)

You created your Ad set, next you need to create your ad. For that, select Ads menu above and click on the + button

Select the existing campaign, exiting ad set, name your new ad

and click on Create

The next page will look like this

1) Select your fan page

2) Select Existing Post and select your post

3) Select the conversion pixel

Step 4) Upload and Save changes

Then just go to the top and click on the "Upload Changes"

TWISTER

We found something else, and with a little variation to the ad above we were able to get 3X more clicks, 2X more leads and double our profits.

What is it?

We tried to test our luck with mobile ads and BOOM! We found a goldmine. Not only we got 3X more clicks than Desktop Newsfeed ads, but we generated 2X more leads and 2X more profits.

But it didn't happen on our very first try, we made a few

mistakes. But you won't make those mistakes because I am

going to show you what I did exactly...

What to do now?

Create a new Ad set, use the same old existing campaign (or new campaign whatever u prefer)

Name your ad set like before – add android for tracking purpose, select your conversion pixel. Click create

Scroll down below to placement and select just Mobile News

Feed.

Select Android devices only and tick only when connected to

Wi-Fi. (You can try iOS also, but Android did much better for us, if try iOS, create a new ad set for that to test)

Keep the audience the same, and adjust your budget according to the audience size (the table I gave you earlier in the course). Then create a new ad, select your post, upload and done.

*Note: While running mobile ads, make sure you CPA offers are mobile optimized and they pay for mobile traffic.

This is exactly what I am talking about. Also make sure your

landing pages are mobile optimized. (Instabuilder pages are mobile friendly)

Also, keep testing your landing pages for higher conversions.

What's next?

Repeat the ad creation process till you have created 4-6 ad sets with different interests to test.

(Keep budget for each interest between $5-$15 depending on the size of audience)

Keep everything else same and you are good to go.

Additional Tip:

If you're looking to add just buyers to your list, then this will help. Select behaviors while creating your ad, select Digital Activities => FB Payments (All).

This will just target the people who have made any purchases while they were logged into the Facebook ;)

Let your ads run for 24 hrs. (full day) at least before removing

any ads. Facebook takes at least 2-3 days to optimize your ads and then your "Cost Per Conversion" will start getting lower.

So don't just stop your ads if you see them costing a lot in the

first few hours.

Let your ads run at least 24 hours before making a decision.

Module 5 – Optimizing and Scaling

Tip 1: Scale Out Don't Scale Up

Once you have found a few good ad sets, don't increase the budget to like from $5 to $50. This will only result in you paying more as Facebook will think that you have a large budget and they will start charging you more.

Do it step wise, every 2-3 days $5-$10, $10-$20, $20-$30, $30-

$50. (Increase your budget by 100-150% only)

Add more interests and again repeat the above steps you'll do fine. Target people according to the device (mobile, computer) they use, age groups, sex, countries – keeping the same interest.

Save all the interests that's performing well for you to use later.

What works best for me?

I create many different Website conversion ads at a $5 daily budget. While creating my Ads, these are a few things I make sure of:

Audience size – minimum 1,000,000 (add different interests till they add up to 1,000,000 or higher)

If it's more I just break them down to small audience sizes, like

breakdown one 2,000,000 audience to two 1,000,000 audience sizes.

Run website conversion ads for both desktop newsfeed and mobile devices. See which is performing best for you and making you more profits. If I get a positive ROI, I just keep running them.

I keep adding 4-6 website conversion ads each day with $5, $7 budget. See they how they perform after 2-3 days and stop the ones not performing well and keep the ones doing well.

Don't raise the budget, just let them run. Once the frequency of

ads reaches like 1.4 I stop them and run new ads.

Tip 2: Lookalike Audiences

You can create audiences based on your Retargeting audience, conversion pixel or email list. You need to have minimum of

100 people in your audience before you can create a lookalike audience.

Go here: https://www.facebook.com/ads/audience _manager

Keep the audience as low as possible, will be more targeted

Tip 3: What matters the most is ROI

One thing you should understand is that some niches will cost you more than others. But it doesn't mean you should stop running your ads. What matters the most is ROI's.

Even if you are paying $1 per click/view but you are making

$200 or even $150 every $100 you spend then you will keep running those ads right.

Tip 4: Retargeting, vital

Make sure you have a retargeting pixel on your landing pages. No matter what, make sure you are retargeting. These lists are super targeted as they have already shown interest in your ad. And when you run ads to them they are much cheaper, highly targeted and convert way better.

Remember an average person needs to see something at least

7 times before they buy it and retargeting does just that.

Once you have a huge re-targeting list, you can keep promoting related offers to them. Makes sense?

Results with NEW ads for last 24 hrs

My results with new ads. I ran these for just 24 hrs and they are not yet optimized (removing the not performing ads)

Once I optimize them and ad more campaigns, I

will be making over $100 in profits each day.

The last didn't perform well, as I forgot to select android devices. So make sure you don't forget that like I did.

Below are my results for another campaign.

So, for today I spent $46.26 (with bad ads included)

Profits = $89 - $46.26 = $42.74

So, I just need to add 2 more campaigns like the ones I already have, remove the non-performing ones and I will be on my way to $100/day with this new campaign □

So there you have it!

Stop reading and start working.

Conclusion

Making money with CPA is an exciting venture to a part of, especially as you are able to earn money without having to sell products or recruit customers. For many, this factor alone is the very reason why they choose to be a part of the CPA industry, rather than regular affiliate marketing.

The CPA guide was written to provide an introduction to CPA, and I encourage you to continue learning about the networks, and options available to you.

If you wish to be as successful as you can be, then you will need to stay on top of industry trends, hot topics and popular subjects, and the easiest way to do that is to get involved in CPA based forums, groups and communities.